Changing Europe

Challenges Facing the Voluntary and Community Sectors in the 1990s

Sean Baine, John Benington and Jill Russell

COMMUNITY
DEVELOPMENT
FOUNDATION

NCVO Publications and Community Development Foundation

Published by NCVO Publications
(incorporating Bedford Square Press)
imprint of the
National Council for Voluntary Organisations
26 Bedford Square, London WC1B 3HU and by
Community Development Foundation
60 Highbury Grove, London N5 2AG

First published 1992
Reprinted 1993

Typeset in house
Printed and bound in Great Britain by J.W. Arrowsmith Ltd, Bristol
Cover printed by The Heyford Press, Wellingborough

A catalogue record for this book is available from the British Library.

ISBN 0 7199 1328 4

CHANGING EUROPE

Challenges Facing the Voluntary and Community Sectors in the 1990s

Sean Baine is currently a Research Associate at
The Local Government Centre, University of
Warwick. He is also a freelance management
consultant to local government and the
voluntary and community sectors. He has
previously worked as a Chief Officer in two
London Boroughs - Neighbourhood Chief
Executive in Tower Hamlets, and Director of
Leisure Services in Hackney. Prior to that, he
worked in community development and in the
voluntary sector.

John Benington is Director of The Local
Government Centre at the University of
Warwick. He was previously at the Institute of
Local Government Studies at the University of
Birmingham, where he lectured in policy
analysis and management. He has 10 years'
experience of senior management in local
government, most recently as Head of the
Department of Employment & Economic
Development in Sheffield, and 5 years as
Director of the Home Office Community
Development Project in Coventry. He has
been one of the UK Evaluators for the
European Programmes to Combat Poverty
since 1985. He is also joint editor of the
quarterly journal *Local Government Policy
Making.*

Jill Russell job-shares as a Principal Research
Officer at the London Research Centre, and
also undertakes freelance research and writing
on social policy issues. While conducting the
research for this book, she has been based at
The Local Government Centre, University of
Warwick, as a Research Associate. Previously,
she worked at University College Cardiff as
evaluator of a local voluntary project in the
second European Programme to Combat
Poverty. She has also worked for the Coronary
Prevention Group and on other research
projects involving issues of health and social
policy in the voluntary sector.

NCVO Practical Guides

Europe series:

Grants from Europe: How to Get Money and Influence Policy

Networking in Europe: A Guide to European Voluntary Organisations

Other titles in the series:

Artists in Schools: A Handbook for Teachers and Artists
But Is It Legal? Fundraising and the Law
Getting into Print: An Introduction to Publishing
Industrial Tribunals and Appeals: Everything You Need to Know
Opening the Town Hall Door: An Introduction to Local Government, 2nd ed
Organising Your Finances: A Guide to Good Practice
Responding to Child Abuse: Action and Planning for Teachers and Other Professionals
Seeing It Through: How to Be Effective on a Committee
Starting and Running a Voluntary Group
Using the Media, 2nd ed
Who's Having Your Baby?: A Health Rights Handbook for Maternity Care
Working Effectively: A Guide to Evaluation Techniques
You are the Governor: How to be Effective in Your Local School

All books are available through bookshops and can be purchased from NCVO Reception during office hours. To order by post, please contact the NCVO Sales Office for further details.

CONTENTS

PART ONE

Introduction

1   The European Context

2   The Voluntary and Community Sectors and Europe: Setting the Scene

v

PART TWO

3 Economic Change, Employment and Training

4 Social Welfare, Poverty and Disadvantage

5 Black and Ethnic Minorities, and Refugees

6 Women

7 Health

8 The Environment

9 Consumers

PART THREE

10 Summing up the Issues

Appendices

LIST OF DIAGRAMS, BOXES AND TABLES

Tables

FOREWORD

This publication is about the social impact of the Single European Market and the challenges and opportunities it presents to voluntary and community organisations in Britain. We hope that it will be useful in helping these organisations prepare for the consequences of the single market and, in particular, to understand how it will affect, for better or worse, the communities and groups that are assisted by voluntary and community bodies.

The publication is based upon research commissioned by the National Council for Voluntary Organisations (NCVO) and the Community Development Foundation (CDF) from The Local Government Centre at the University of Warwick. The research was directed by John Benington and carried out by Sean Baine, Oonagh McDonald and Jill Russell. We are grateful to them for their diligence and careful analysis of the material. We are also indebted to the Advisory Committee that guided the project. Its members are listed in Appendix A on page 155.

Our thanks go to the Joseph Rowntree Foundation for their generous financial support, and for the active participation of its research director, Janet Lewis, in the work of the study.

Finally, we acknowledge the important contribution of Gabriel Chanan, Marilyn Taylor, Bill Seary and Nigel Tarling.

Judy Weleminsky
Director, NCVO

David Thomas
Chief Executive, CDF

ACKNOWLEDGEMENTS

The research team would like to thank the Joseph Rowntree Foundation for funding this project, and in particular Janet Lewis (Research Director of the Foundation) for her commitment and advice throughout the research. NCVO and CDF sponsored and actively supported the research, and members of the advisory committee (Appendix A) were generous in the time they gave to commenting on the research programme and successive drafts of this report. We are particularly grateful for the perspectives provided by Bill Seary, Marilyn Taylor, Gabriel Chanan and David Thomas. Other people who gave helpful comments on the drafts were Diana Robbins, Roger Watkins, Imogen Sharp, Jeanette Longfield, Brian Harvey, Don Flynn, Stephen Crampton and colleagues at The Local Government Centre, University of Warwick.

We also want to acknowledge the contribution made by Oonagh McDonald who carried out the initial interviews and a literature survey which provided a foundation for the later research.

The research team is also grateful to all the people and organisations who shared information, views and ideas with us on the social impact of the single European market. Appendix B contains a list of all the people and organisations who contributed in this way. Victoria Winkler, Diana Robbins, Brian Harvey, Bill Seary and the Euro-Citizen-Action-Service also kindly provided material for some of the boxes and appendices in this report.

The report would never have been completed without the excellent and patient secretarial support of Maureen Causby at The Local Government Centre. Rosie Leyden of Wordworks helped at very short notice with the editing of this report and we are grateful to her.

Finally, Jill Russell would also like to thank Charles Sweeney for his patience during the long hours it took to prepare this report and Chris Russell for her interest, advice and much more.

Sean Baine, John Benington, Jill Russell
The Local Government Centre, University of Warwick
August 1991

ABBREVIATIONS

BEUG	European Bureau of Consumer Unions
CAP	Common Agricultural Policy
CDF	Community Development Foundation
CECG	Consumers in the European Community Group
EAPN	European Anti Poverty Network
EC	European Community
ECAS	Euro-Citizen-Action-Service
ECU	European Currency Unit
EEB	European Environmental Bureau
EFTA	European Free Trade Association
ENOW	European Network of Women
ERM	Exchange Rate Mechanism
ERDF	European Regional Development Fund
ESAN	European Social Action Network
ESF	European Social Fund
EWL	European Women's Lobby
FEANTSA	European Federation of National Organisations Working with the Homeless
GDP	Gross Domestic Product
IHN	International Heart Network
MEP	Member of the European Parliament
NCVO	National Council for Voluntary Organisations
NGO	Non-governmental Organisation
RADAR	Royal Association for Disability and Rehabilitation
RNIB	Royal National Institute for the Blind
RNID	Royal National Institute for the Deaf
PHA	Public Health Alliance
SEA	Single European Act
SPAN	Single Parent Action Network
WHO	World Health Organisation

PART ONE

INTRODUCTION

THE AIMS OF THE REPORT

The purpose of this report is to analyse the implications of the single European market, and related developments in the European Community (EC), for voluntary and community organisations in the UK.

Europe is clearly at a crucial turning-point in its history. The profound changes that have been taking place in political and economic regimes, in the boundaries between nation states, and in the relationships between Eastern and Western Europe, amount to one of the most significant watersheds since the Second World War.

The movement towards economic, monetary and political union within the EC seems to be gathering momentum at such a rapid pace that some commentators have argued that it is conceivable that by the end of the decade the UK will be part of a United States of Europe, with an elected European president, and with a new European currency, the European Currency Unit (ECU), standing alongside the dollar and the yen, as one of the three main world currencies.

Within this canvas of larger-scale and longer-term changes, the moves towards a single market between the 12 member states of the EC is having major repercussions for economic and social policy in the UK. 1992, and all that goes with it, is changing the context within which the public, private, voluntary and community sectors have traditionally operated in the UK.

In this report the following questions are addressed:

- What are the implications of these far-reaching European changes for the policies and work of voluntary and community organisations at national, regional and local level?

- How can voluntary and community organisations best prepare to meet the challenges and opportunities presented by the new Europe?

- How can voluntary and community organisations take advantage of the new cross-national networks and the new political processes emerging, to influence the development and shape of European social policies?

3

THE METHODS OF ENQUIRY

In order to gain as full an understanding as possible of the challenges facing voluntary and community organisations in the Europe of the 1990s, the research for this report combined several methods of enquiry. These included:

- The collection and analysis of a growing literature on the socio-economic impact of 1992. Appendix E contains a selection of the material we found most useful, including some of the regular bulletins about Europe, produced specifically for the voluntary and community sectors.

- Consultation with a range of experts (policy-makers, lobbyists, academics, etc.) on developments in the EC, both in the UK and in Brussels. This also included regular discussions with our research advisory committee (Appendix A) and the three sponsoring organisations (NCVO, CDF and the Joseph Rowntree Foundation).

- A survey of ideas and opinions about 1992 in the voluntary and community sectors. This study represents the first attempt in the UK to canvass the views of voluntary and community organisations about the impact and implications of the single European market, about the levels of involvement in European activities which they are finding most useful, and about their views on ways forward.

Appendix B contains greater detail of the methods used, and identifies the organisations and individuals who generously contributed to this research.

The combination of different methods and levels of enquiry (local, regional, national and European) enabled us to get beyond a one-dimensional picture, and to develop a deeper understanding of some of the challenges facing the voluntary and community sectors in the Europe of the 1990s. However, it is clear that European policies and initiatives are developing at a considerable pace, and this report can only provide one perspective on the picture that has emerged in mid-1991. The pattern is likely to alter as the kaleidoscope of European change moves on again. In addition, a single piece of research cannot do justice to the richness and diversity of experience contained within the voluntary and community sectors. What is presented here, then, can only be a snapshot of the European changes and challenges facing voluntary and community organisations in the UK at the time of writing, and our interpretation of current trends.

THE FRAMEWORK FOR THE REPORT

Chapter 1 examines the developments and debates, and the competing interests and ideas, which are shaping the large-scale changes in Europe, and which are influencing the shifting balance of forces between a more competitive European market and a more cohesive European community. It aims to give the reader a brief introduction to the economic, social and political dimensions of the Europe in which voluntary and community organisations will be working in the forthcoming years.

Chapter 2 identifies the changing and often conflicting roles and functions of voluntary and community organisations in the UK, and introduces the reader to some of the possible impacts that a more integrated and competitive Europe may have on the different types of organisation and activity. It also explores how the voluntary and community sectors are currently perceived within Europe, and indicates how the European institutions are increasingly wanting to work with these sectors.

The second part of the report consists of a series of chapters about specific policy themes. They highlight the impact of the single European market upon a selection of issues or groups of people which are particularly relevant to the voluntary and community sectors in the UK. The areas covered are:

Chapter 3:   Economic change, employment and training.
Chapter 4:   Social welfare, poverty and disadvantage.
Chapter 5:   Black and ethnic minorities and refugees.
Chapter 6:   Women.
Chapter 7:   Health.
Chapter 8:   The environment.
Chapter 9:   Consumers.

Time and resources have prevented us from covering all policy areas of interest to voluntary and community organisations. In particular, we have not been able to say much about the impact of the single European market upon education and youth policies, arts and culture, or relations with the developing countries.

In the final part of the report in Chapter 10 we pull together some of the lessons from and for the voluntary and community sectors, and suggest strategies they might pursue to take best advantage of the new challenges and opportunities emerging at a European level.

1

The European Context

INTRODUCTION

In the 1970s and early 1980s the European Economic Community appeared to be in a state of division and confusion.[1] The images on the news were of constant disputes over the EC budget, with increasing amounts of money being swallowed up by the Common Agricultural Policy (CAP), and the UK arguing about the level of its contribution. The UK always appeared to be in a minority of one, blocking agreement on a wide range of matters. Butter mountains and wine lakes threatened, in an almost physical sense, to dominate the rural landscapes of Europe. The economic pundits talked of 'eurosclerosis', a debilitating disease that was eating away at European industrial capability, and leaving the way open for American and Japanese competitors to seize the initiative in world markets.[2]

However, by the early 1990s, while no one can claim that all these problems have been solved, there is a fresh sense of purpose about the European project. The year 1992 is now quoted as a symbol of a new dynamism in European affairs. Expressing this feeling, Jacques Delors, the President of the Commission, has predicted that by the year 2000 the EC will become responsible for some '80 per cent of economic and social legislation'.[3]

In the midst of all this new-found energy and speculation about the future, it is difficult to distinguish between reality and wishful thinking. The Gulf War in 1990-1991 raised important questions about some of the grander claims concerning political and military co-operation in the Europe of the future. There are feelings in the UK that the EC failed to achieve political and diplomatic unity in the face of Iraq's invasion of Kuwait. Yet the divisions between the 12 member states may have been just the impetus that was required to move towards greater European unity in order to avoid such disunity coming to the surface in the future.[4] Inter-governmental conferences

7

have been meeting to discuss steps towards further European union, and at the time of writing (June 1991) it was reported that proposals would be brought forward for a common EC foreign and security policy, and greater powers for the European Parliament.

In the UK, the change of Prime Minister in November 1990 appeared to herald a change in the Government's attitude to the EC. In a key speech in March 1991 the new Prime Minister, John Major, said:

> My aims for Britain in the Community can be simply stated: I want us to be where we belong. At the very heart of Europe. Working with our partners in building the future. This is a challenge we take up with enthusiasm.[5]

Yet, while a change of tone or even attitude may be taking place, it is still unclear what this will mean in practice. On individual policies such as the Social Charter (page 18) and monetary union, little seems to have changed in the British government's position. If there is significant progress towards greater union then the UK will be forced to choose between being part of that greater union or staying isolated. In particular, there may be a conflict between the UK's traditional special relationship with the United States and closer ties with Europe.

So, what is the likely shape of the EC in the 1990s? What is the European context in which voluntary and community organisations will be working in the forthcoming years? To answer these questions this chapter looks at Europe from three perspectives. First, it examines economic Europe and the ideas behind 1992 and the single European market. It then looks at social Europe and tries to judge how far ideas about integration have advanced beyond the purely economic. Finally it examines the idea of a political Europe and describes developments towards wider integration.

ECONOMIC EUROPE

The Treaty of Rome and the Single European Act

The original Treaty of Rome establishing the European Economic Community was signed in 1957. According to Article Two of the Treaty:

> The Community shall have as its task, by establishing a common market and progressively approximating the economic policies of member states, to promote throughout the Community a harmonious development of economic activities, a continuous and balanced

expansion, an increase in stability, an accelerated raising of the standard of living and closer relations between the States belonging to it.[6]

This was to be achieved by a number of measures such as the elimination of customs barriers, the establishment of common customs tariffs and the abolition of obstacles to freedom of movement for persons, services and capital.

For a variety of economic and political reasons the Treaty was never fully implemented. However, during the early 1980s, economic stagnation, lack of growth, continuing high levels of unemployment, and an increasing awareness of the superiority of the American and Japanese economies, particularly in the area of new technologies, provided the impetus for change.[7] The 1985 White Paper[8] outlined the Commission's strategy for the completion of a single European market and was accepted by all the European heads of government. The proposals in the White Paper were incorporated in the Single European Act (SEA), which came into operation on 1 July 1987.[9] Member states committed themselves to adopting all the various measures outlined in the SEA by 30 December 1992 - hence the shorthand use of '1992' to describe the process and the programme.

How Will a Single European Market Be Achieved?

The economic measures that are part of the move to a single market can be summarised under the following headings:

- **Elimination of barriers to transborder business activity.** This applies in areas such as capital movements, banking, insurance, telecommunications and transport. Different regulations in the different countries have made operating at a European level very difficult.

- **Reduction in fiscal barriers.** At present indirect taxes such as VAT and excise duties vary considerably between member states. It is proposed to achieve as much convergence as possible.

- **Increase in the mobility of labour.** One way in which it is intended to achieve this is through the mutual recognition of professional qualifications.

- **Abolition of physical barriers.** For example, the elimination of passport checks for people and customs documentation for goods. There will be simplified procedures for export-import documents.

- **Reduction of technical barriers in respect of product regulations, health and safety and cultural values.** Having many different requirements in the different countries means extra costs for manufacturers trying to export their goods to other member states. There are also additional research and development costs. In some areas, such as health and safety, the approach of the EC will be to aim at harmonisation[10] and the issuing of mandatory requirements. In other areas, an alternative approach of mutual recognition will increasingly be used: that is, if a product can be sold in one member state it can also be sold in all other EC countries.

- **Abolition of government protectionism in procurement.** This means eliminating those practices of national and local governments which give preference to their own national and local supplies in the awarding of new contracts (for example, for telecommunications equipment). All contracts over a certain amount will have to be advertised at a European level (page 34) and government subsidies to home industries will be stopped.

In addition to the above economic measures, the SEA also amended decision-making procedures within the EC, but these will be dealt with later in the section on political Europe.

The Effects of the Single European Market

The effects of the reduction or abolition of all these barriers is intended to be a supply-side shock to the European economy. This means that industry will be shaken up by greater competition and by the removal of protective tariffs and subsidies. The proponents of the SEA expect this shock to bring four main results:

- **New patterns of competition,** in which 'over-capacity' will be eliminated, and weaker firms will be eliminated or taken over.

- **A significant reduction in costs** due to economies of scale, and the elimination of bureaucratic procedures and paperwork involved in exporting to member states, and the reduction in the costs of developing different products for different countries.

- **Improved efficiency in companies** as prices move downwards in response to more competition.

- **Increased innovation** and the development of new products created by the dynamics of the new market.

All of this is intended to make European industry more competitive both within Europe and in export markets. Falling costs, it is argued, will be reflected in lower prices for the consumer.

The benefits of a single market were calculated by a group of EC experts led by an Italian economist, Paolo Cecchini. The Cecchini Committee supervised and directed a vast research programme into the economics of the European market: the much-quoted Cecchini Report contains a summary of the findings of this programme.[11] The effects of increased market integration, as predicted by the Cecchini Committee, are outlined in Box A (page 12). The committee calculated that the net gains from removing trade barriers would amount to approximately 200 billion ECUs (approximately £140 billion). These gains are detailed in Table 1.

Table 1

POTENTIAL GAINS IN ECOMONIC WELFARE FOR THE EC RESULTING FROM COMPLETION OF THE INTERNAL MARKET

	Billions ECU	% of GDP
Step 1 Gains from removal of barriers affecting trade.	8-9	0.2-0.3
Step 2 Gains from removal of barriers affecting overall production.	57-71	2.0-2.4
Gains from removing barriers (sub-total).	65-80	2.2-2.7
Step 3 Gains from exploiting economies of scale more fully.	61	2.1
Step 4 Gains from intensified competition reducing business inefficiencies and monopoly profits.	46	1.6
Gains from market integration (sub-total).	62*-107	2.1*-3.7
Total for		
7 Member States at 1985 prices.	127-187	4.3-6.4
12 Member States at 1988 prices.	174-258	4.3-6.4
Mid-point of above.	216	5.3

*   This alternative estimate for the sum of steps 3 and 4 cannot be broken down between the two steps.

Source: Cecchini, P. (1988), *The European Challenge: 1992 The Benefits of a Single Market*, Wildwood House

PRINCIPAL MACRO-ECONOMIC MECHANISMS ACTIVATED IN THE COURSE OF COMPLETING THE INTERNAL MARKET

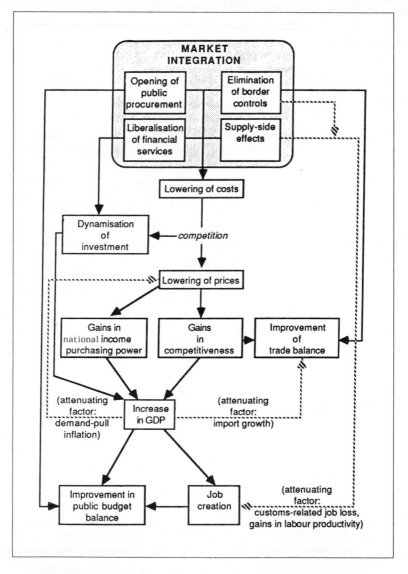

Source: Cecchini, P. (1988), *The European Challenge: 1992 The Benefits of a Single Market*, Wildwood House

In Table 1, the ranges for certain lines represent the results of using alternative sources of information and methodologies. The seven member states (Germany, France, Italy, United Kingdom, Benelux) account for 88% of the GDP of the EC twelve. Extrapolation of the results in terms of the same share of GDP for the seven and twelve Member States is not likely to over-estimate the total for the twelve. The detailed figures in the table relate only to the seven Member States because the underlying studies mainly covered those countries.

Although the end of 1992 has been given as the target for implementing all the measures, the process is already well under way. By April 1990, about 60 per cent of the 1992 programme had been adopted and the Commission had produced proposals in all areas. A total of 282 new measures have been proposed, but some member states have been slow in implementing the measures. Despite what might be expected by its general attitudes to the Community, the UK is at the top of the implementation league table, having implemented 77 measures by February 1990.

Even the proponents of the single market accept that the effects will not necessarily be uniformly good. The worries are that 1992 will lead to the rationalisation of industry and in the short-term will mean job losses in some areas. These job losses are expected to be concentrated in particular industries. For example, it is accepted that there is over-production by several European manufacturing industries. If there is to be contraction, some areas that are dependent on these industries could be badly affected. It is suggested that new industry is likely to be concentrated in what is called the 'golden triangle', bounded by London, Frankfurt and Milan. If this is the case then regions on the periphery of the Community such as the north of England, Scotland, Wales and Northern Ireland could suffer to an even greater extent. These issues will be explored in more depth in Chapter 3.

Some critics claim that the effects of the single market have been exaggerated. According to Grahl and Teague:

> there tends to be an exaggerated stress on tariffs and equivalent governmental measures as obstacles to international exchange, to the neglect of the social divergences which sustain separate national economies quite independently of protectionist policies.[12]

So, while there may be important effects for large industries which already operate at a transnational level, this is not necessarily true for large numbers of medium and small enterprises, especially in the service industries, where the effects may be much less than predicted. According to this view the barriers of language and culture are likely to retain their importance in the foreseeable future, and change will only occur if there are significant changes in the behaviour of a number of groups, such as individual consumers, families and small businesses. However, even if medium- and small-sized businesses do not expand their operations into Europe, they may still be affected by changes in the overall economic context as a result of 1992. For example, small-scale suppliers of components to the motor industry will be affected by any rationalisation of the industry at a European level.

The 1992 programme is essentially a deregulatory programme. It concentrates mainly on what might be called negative integration, i.e. the removal of barriers to trade and enterprise. It is these aspects which have received the whole-hearted support of the Conservative government in the UK. However, there are also strong arguments in favour of more positive integration. The deregulatory nature of the programme will bring into play a new set of economic forces, all the more powerful for operating at the European level and across national boundaries. So, it is argued, there is a need for a counterbalance to be provided by the European institutions. This would take two forms: unified monetary management, and providing a more significant *social* dimension to European integration.

The discussion on unified monetary management centres on two main ideas: a single currency and a European Central Bank.

At present the different exchange rates are seen to be a considerable barrier to trade, because of their possible fluctuations, as well as the expense of changing from one currency to another. It has been calculated that if a person started with £100 and changed the money into the local currency of every EC country visited, there would only be £28 left at the end of the journey, due to the cost of changing currency![13]

The Exchange Rate Mechanism (ERM) limits the extent to which the 12 EC currencies can change in value against each other. This reduces uncertainty but still leaves scope for the re-alignment of individual currencies. The plan for full monetary union would involve abolishing national currencies and having a single European currency. The British government has put forward different proposals that would mean turning the ECU into a thirteenth Community currency, which could be used in all parts of the EC but which would not threaten national currencies. With a single currency there would be a European Central Bank, which would manage the currency, set interest rates, and regulate the conduct of financial services such as insurance throughout the Community.

There are concerns that a single currency would be of more benefit to the richer countries. Poorer areas would not be able to lower the value of their currencies to help them compete with the richer countries. They could be faced with a prolonged period of slow economic growth while they lowered their costs. There are also concerns in the UK and in other countries that there would be a loss of sovereignty, as control of currency matters would pass to a non-elected European Central Bank, which might take decisions against the interests of individual states.

One way of counterbalancing the destabilising effects of a more competitive European market may be to move to a common monetary policy. But a second way, and perhaps one with more direct relevance to the voluntary and community sectors, is to provide a significant *social* dimension to European integration.

SOCIAL EUROPE

Some people would like to see 1992 as no more than the creation of a single trading zone, and the Europe of 1992 as the 'Europe of competition'. Such commentators warn of the need to be 'vigilant and beware of Eurobureaucrats' who wish to see the powers of the EC extended beyond the purely economic.[14] On the other hand, there are those who argue that a more competitive and integrated European market will not benefit all sectors of the population, and believe that the EC has a responsibility to develop social policies to counteract these divisive effects and to enhance social cohesion throughout the member states.[15]

The Forces for a Social Europe

A number of problems in the functioning of the new European economic order have been highlighted by those calling for a strong social dimension to European unity. These are discussed in detail in Chapters 3 and 4, and include:

- Increased job-loss and unemployment (at least in the short-term) as a result of the restructuring of industry.

- An increase in regional disparities as the London-Frankfurt-Milan triangle attracts the growth industries and new investment.

- Labour shortfalls in the new skills that will be required by the new industries and inadequate opportunities for retraining.

- Social dumping, i.e. the fear that in a situation where barriers to free trade are removed but disparities between the member states remain, firms and employers will be attracted to those countries with the lowest labour and social costs, and, conversely, that the poor will have an incentive to move to those countries or regions with the most generous welfare and social security systems.

- The needs of a growing number of poor, marginalised or excluded people in Europe.

In addition, demographic changes are leading to a higher dependency ratio and, in particular, to much higher numbers of elderly people.

The move towards a social dimension also has been supported by the entry of the southern European countries of Spain, Portugal and Greece to the EC. These countries are much poorer than the original members and have provided a substantial pressure towards equalisation of social benefits. They also have altered the balance of where any social expenditure might go. Ten years ago the UK might have expected to be a net beneficiary of redistributed funds, but now the beneficiaries will be Spain, Portugal, Greece, Southern Italy and Ireland. This has been a significant factor in the British government's opposition to any increases in the Community budget.

In exploring the social dimension of the EC it is important to understand that to date the Commission has largely used the term 'social policy' to refer to policies concerned with the living and working conditions of workers rather than citizens. In most member states social policy has a much broader definition and encompasses a mass of welfare policy and legislation directed at all categories of people, not just at workers. However, because the original European treaties were for the setting up of a European economic community, EC social policies have been focused on protecting the rights of workers in relation to employment, rather than their rights as citizens in relation to their social needs.

A growing body of opinion is critical of the way in which EC social policy is so narrowly focused, and wants to see an extension of the EC's legal competence into the field of social welfare. Much of what the voluntary and community sectors (and sometimes the Commission and European Parliament) would like the Community to take a stand on, or put resources into, is not possible because the EC's powers of legal 'competence' lie almost entirely in the economic arena. Having said this, there is a body of opinion that believes the Commission has used the limited competence argument as an excuse for not getting involved in areas it does not want to. Social housing and homelessness have been cited as examples of issues where, if the political will existed, the Commission could in fact find a legal basis for action.

In the light of the continuing discussion about extending the competence of the Community, the Euro-Citizen-Action-Service (see Box E in Chapter 2 for a description of this organisation) has prepared a memorandum on possible revisions to the European treaties that they believe would benefit the work of voluntary and community organisations. The main areas are outlined in Box B. The future of representations such as these, and the final decisions taken by the Council of Ministers, will be of crucial importance to the voluntary and community sectors and their relationship with Europe.

There are three main strands to the existing development of social policy within the Community: the Structural Funds, the Social Charter, and various action and research programmes.

BOX B

REVISION OF THE EC TREATIES

The Euro-Citizen-Action-Service (ECAS) argues that:

1   The powers of the European Parliament must be strengthened, to enable this institution which has always been most responsive to citizens' demands to initiate not only spending but new legislation too.

2   The revision of the Treaty must end artificial limitations on EC competence. Under the SEA, chapters were added on social cohesion, environment and research. Civil liberties, public health and culture should be included now.

3   The new Treaty should provide guidelines for applying the principle of 'subsidiarity' to new areas (i.e. limiting the EC to action with a genuine European dimension). There is danger of this principle being misused to block social progress.

4   Under the new Treaty, the role of citizens' associations in the non-profit sector should be included rather than excluded in the chapters on right of establishment and freedom to provide services. A European Statute for Associations is required to enable them to operate easily across borders, on the basis of Treaty articles recognising their social objectives.

5   Citizens' associations in the voluntary sector should be recognised in the Treaty alongside employers and trade unions as a social partner. A forum to consult the voluntary social economy sector is needed just as much as one for local authorities. The Community should provide better means to handle citizens' complaints and to facilitate their access to national courts and the European Court on EC matters.

6   The EC should become a party to the European convention on human rights and its responsibility extended to civil liberties as the European Parliament demands. Decisions affecting the rights of refugees and immigrants from third countries must be included in Community competence and brought under democratic control.

7   There 'should be a general provision outlawing discrimination, not only on the grounds of nationality, but also on grounds of race, sex, disability and age. Article 119 of the EC Treaty provides for application of the principle that men and women should receive equal pay for equal work. This provision should be extended to other people who suffer discrimination in access to employment, pay, and living conditions.

8   The EC should have competence for public health measures in the Treaty. This would mean legislative initiatives on medicines, food and environmental protection should be justified on public health grounds and not only to eliminate trade barriers. As the Commission proposes, a legal basis is needed for EC campaigns to combat cancer, AIDS, cardio-vascular disease and drug abuse.

9   The titles on social policy should be strengthened and extended to cover living as well as working conditions. The new Treaty should provide a basis for legislative action, not just non-binding recommendations and financial support in favour of child welfare, elderly, disabled and poor people. There should be specific provision on consumer protection in the Treaty.

10 Cultural policy should be added to the Treaty to ensure the protection of minority cultures, the promotion of European cultural events and media policy, and the taking into account of culture in other countries.

Source: *The European Citizen*, January 1991

The Structural Funds

The main instruments of a Social Europe to date are what have come to be called the Structural Funds (previously operating as three separate funds - the Social Fund, Regional Fund, and part of the Agricultural Guidance and Guarantee Fund). These Funds support projects to improve the infrastucture of the poorer regions in the EC, rural development schemes, and employment and training initiatives. The Structural Funds are described in Chapter 3.

The Social Charter

Many people have recognised the limitations of what can be done at the European level within existing powers and limited budgets. Perhaps the most ambitious proposal to date to make significant progress in this area has been the adoption of the Social Charter in December 1989 by 11 of the member states - the exception being the UK. The Social Charter (formally called the

Community Charter of Fundamental Social Rights) is a 'solemn declaration' by the signatories. This means that it has no legal status but that the signatories are morally and politically committed to guarantee the social rights contained in the Charter. The Charter is essentially a charter of workers' rights, although it includes areas previously untouched by EC social policy, such as elderly people, social protection (i.e. welfare benefits) and the protection of children. Rights covered by the Charter are outlined in Box C.

BOX C

THE SOCIAL CHARTER

The Community Charter of Fundamental Social Rights, often referred to as the Social Charter, outlines the following rights that the signatories are committed to implement.

1　The right to freedom of movement within the Community for every worker.

2　The right to be free to choose an occupation and to be fairly remunerated.

3　The right to improved living and working conditions.

4　The right of each worker to adequate social protection and an adequate level of social security benefits.

5　The right of employers and employees to join together to defend their interests and the right to resort to collective action.

6　The right of every worker to have access to vocational training throughout their working life.

7　The right of men and women to be treated equally.

8　The rights of workers to be informed and consulted about, and to participate in, decisions affecting their work.

9　The right to satisfactory health and safety conditions in the working environment.

10　The right of every worker, upon retirement, to the resources that give him or her a decent standard of living.

11　The right of all disabled persons to additional concrete measures to improve their social and professional integration.

Source: CEC (1990) *The Community Charter of Fundamental Social Rights for Workers*, European File, June 1990

The Commission has agreed an action programme of measures to fulfil the rights outlined in the Social Charter.[16] It sees this programme as:

> ...more than an inventory of measures. It represents the backbone of Commission initiatives for the next three years in the social domain... it demonstrates the reality of the social dimension of the internal market - an ambitious objective - but not blanket harmonisation...[17]

Others are less optimistic. The European Parliament was disappointed with the final text of the Charter and wished to see its scope expanded to include areas such as the right to a minimum income and social protection for all. Several governments also wanted it strengthened, including the German government, but others, the most prominent of which was the British government, did not. The British government's position is that:

> ... it supports the principle of Community action in areas where there is a clear need for European standards, eg health and safety at work, free movement of workers. However the Government believes that many other areas covered in the Charter and now in the action programme are best left to national or local agreement, eg regulation of part-time and temporary work, working laws and worker participation.[18]

Within the current EC decision-making procedures, all proposals relating to the Charter, except those concerned with health and safety, have to receive the unanimous agreement of member states. The opposition of primarily the British government to many of the proposals is therefore preventing or delaying their implementation. Nevertheless, many in the Commission are hopeful that qualified majority voting (page 22) will soon be extended to the whole of the social affairs field, which would effectively enable the complete Social Charter to be incorporated into legislation.

Action and Research Programmes

The Commission supports a growing number of smaller programmes aimed at specific issues or groups of people. Examples are the European programmes to combat poverty (page 80), the HELIOS programme for people with disabilities (page 86), and the IRIS programme bringing together projects undertaking vocational training for women (Box L, Chapter 6). These programmes are primarily concerned with the funding of demonstration projects, networks and databases, spreading information and good practice. While they clearly have some value as catalysts for local and national developments, their impact on mainstream policies may be limited because of their small scale, which in turn is partly a consequence of the limited competence of the EC to act in such areas. Part Two of this report explores the value of these programmes in greater detail.

In addition to action programmes, a number of 'observatories' and research programmes/networks have been established on, for example, the family, and poverty (Chapter 4). The function of observatories is - as the name implies - to maintain a watching brief on a particular area of policy, to highlight trends, and to indentify the European dimension. The funding of observatories and other research work relates to the Commission's strategy of improving European collaboration and intra-EC learning on social policy issues through exchange and synthesis of information about research and policy. Observatories and research also provide a way for the Commission to become more involved in areas of social policy, particularly where limited competence prevents more active involvement.[19]

Small as these action and research programmes are, they may hold the key to the future development of social policy within the Community. Whether they do or not will ultimately depend on political considerations about the future shape of Europe.

POLITICAL EUROPE

The EC is a unique international organisation in that legislation it enacts can override national legislation and can be enforced by a judicial system that is above the judicial systems of the individual member states. The EC also has independent budgetary resources in the form of an automatic percentage of some indirect taxation (Appendix C) and can take autonomous decisions about its own expenditure. But it is limited in the sense that most of the legislation has to be agreed unanimously by all the members i.e. by each of the national governments. There are now pressures from many of the member states for increased integration of political and security policies. Both the Italian presidency in the second half of 1990 and the Luxembourg presidency in the first half of 1991 (Appendix C) brought forward ambitious plans for a revision of the treaties to allow for economic and monetary union, a common Community foreign and security policy, and greater powers for the European Parliament.

At the time of writing, a draft treaty had just been presented. In the UK considerable political and media attention was given to the possible use of the word 'federal' in the draft treaty. The British government resisted its use, arguing that a federal government would mean the creation of a centralised super-state and would affect UK sovereignty in an unacceptable way. Other EC governments believe a federal European constitution is more likely to ensure a decentralised, politically pluralist Community than the British alternative of a Europe run by the nation states.[20]

It is likely that a compromise will be reached by the time a new treaty is agreed at the end of 1991. It is possible to speculate that the compromise would allow movement towards economic and monetary union, an increase in majority voting in the Council of Ministers, and an increase in the powers of the Parliament in certain areas, for example, environmental matters. It would not allow any extension of majority voting to social affairs, and the use of the word 'federal' would be dropped .

There is a firm feeling within many of the Community member states that a new target date of 1996 should be set to achieve political union.[21] It is quite likely, therefore, that the British government elected at the next general election will be faced with major decisions on the future shape of the Community, decisions which could change it from an intergovernmental body to a supranational organisation.

The remainder of this section focuses on the EC political process, and in particular on the role of the Council of Ministers and the European Parliament, as in formal terms they are the two key decision-making bodies. The role of the Commission is briefly identified. Appendix C gives a full description of all the Community institutions, and of how decisions are made.

The Commission

The Commission is the only EC institution with the right to initiate proposals for legislation, budgets and programmes of work.[22] As such, it wields a great deal of power, many would say considerably more power than the British Civil Service, and certainly with less accountability. (For a description of the composition and appointment of the Commission see Appendix C.) The Commission's task is also to administer the many EC programmes described in this report, and to monitor the way in which the treaties and subsequent legislation are observed by the member states.[23]

The Council of Ministers

The trend in the 1980s was clearly to increase the power of the Community institutions. The SEA extended the concept of majority voting in the Council of Ministers, the legislature of the Community. This means that, for certain matters, a decision may be taken by a qualified majority (the 'majority procedure'). Under this procedure the votes of the member states are weighted (Appendix C) and two-thirds of the votes can carry a proposal.[24] Unanimous votes are still needed for the more significant proposals, and negotiation is preferred to invoking the majority procedure. As a result, decisions can still take a long time to emerge from various stages of the European process. Decisions made in the Council of Ministers are taken in private, making it the only secret legislature in the democratic world.

The European Parliament

In contrast to the powers of the Council of Ministers, the European Parliament has very limited powers. However, these have been extended by the SEA, which introduced the 'co-operation procedure'. The procedure is a complicated one and involves the Parliament expressing opinions about proposals from the Commission and suggesting amendments to the Commission and the Council of Ministers. Ultimately the Council, if unanimous, can overrule both these bodies. The co-operation procedure only applies to a limited number of articles in the Treaty of Rome, including some social policy legislation and about two-thirds of the internal market proposals. The effect of the new co-operation procedure has been to increase the systematic interaction between the different institutions of the Community and to increase the profile of the European Parliament.

In addition to its limited legislative role, the European Parliament approves the budget of the Community. There are opportunities for lobbying Members of the European Parliament (MEPs) to support particular budget headings (called 'budget lines') that allow particular programmes or new initiatives to go ahead. Several voluntary and community organisations have done so with success (1990 budget lines of interest to voluntary organisations are listed in Box D).

The main role of the European Parliament is therefore not a legislative one. Instead it acts as the conscience of the Community and as a forum for debating its values, direction and priorities. In doing so the Parliament is one of the sources of pressure for extending the role of the Community in social affairs.[25]

It had been hoped that the introduction of elections in which members of the European Parliament were directly elected, rather than nominated by national governments, would give the Parliament a more authoritative voice in the affairs of the Community. However, Denmark is the only member state where the European elections have been fought on European issues. In the others, national issues, involving votes of confidence in the national ruling party of the time, have tended to dominate the European elections. Furthermore, there is no clear-cut division between the major party groupings within the Parliament. The driving force in the European Parliament is currently a coalition between the Socialist and Christian Democrat groups, which hold the great majority of seats and which share the same aspirations for a more unified Europe. Such a coalition is typical of those found in many

1990 BUDGET LINES OF INTEREST TO VOLUNTARY ORGANISATIONS

TITLE	AMOUNT (ECUs)
Subsidies for the defence of human rights	1,995,000
Subsidies to organisations advancing the idea of Europe	775,000
Town-twinning schemes in Europe	3,000,000
Support for international non-governmental youth organisations	420,000
Distribution of agricultural products to deprived persons in the Community	150,000,000
Promotion of interregional co-operation	5,000,000
Business and innovation centres	7,000,000
Tourism-related measures	4,000,000
Youth exchanges	12,400,000
Vocational training and guidance activities	3,650,000
Community measures in favour of minority languages and cultures	1,100,000
Measures and studies in fields of employment and the Community social dimension including specific job creation projects in connection with completion of the internal market	13,500,000
Measures to achieve equality between men and women	2,800,000
Aid to organisations of SMEs	800,000
Measures and studies concerning living and working conditions and social protection including the promotion of social rights in the Community	2,000,000
Measures for disabled persons	5,850,000
Measures for immigrants	4,000,000
Specific Community action to combat poverty	8,140,000
Measures to combat cancer	5,050,000
Measures to combat AIDS	1,100,000
Measures to combat drug abuse	3,900,000
Measures to combat alcohol abuse	1,000,000
Examination and measures in the field of public health	800,000
Action programme on toxicology	360,000
Health protection, hygiene and safety at work	5,100,000
Protection of the environment (large number of separate budgetary lines)	37,760,000
Events in the cultural sector	8,800,000
Sports events for the handicapped	450,000

Information	23,550,000
Consumer protection and information	4,500,000
Grants to European consumer organisations	1,000,000
Child safety	1,600,000
Consumer protection studies	1,000,000
Consumer products safety procedures	200,000
Policy on business, distributive trades, cooperatives, etc	24,300,000
Community contribution towards schemes concerning developing countries carried out by voluntary organisations	85,500,000
Promotion of European public awareness and development education	600,000
Total	**226,560,000**
Overall budget: ECU bn	**46,716**

Source: *European Citizen*, 3 September 1990

of the national governments of the member states and reflects a consensus view of the political process. The UK is a clear exception because of its different voting system, which does not have any element of proportional representation. It is also important to note that many of the Christian Democrat groupings have traditional links with Christian trade union movements and therefore have instinctive sympathy with developments such as the Social Charter. A combination of all these elements means that the UK political parties of both left and right have found difficulty in fitting in with the broader groupings within the European Parliament.[26]

The 'Democratic Deficit'

In spite of the changes outlined above, the institutions of the EC are still not directly accountable to the people of Europe, or their governments. The deficiencies are summed up in the phrase 'the democratic deficit'. This includes concerns about the unaccountable nature of the Council of Ministers, and the limited powers of the European Parliament. It also includes the concern that the President of the Commission and the Commissioners are not elected but nominated by national governments. It is argued that if there are to be moves towards a more political form of union, then the problem of the democratic deficit requires urgent attention.

Subsidiarity

The principle of subsidiarity may play an important part in determining the future shape of political processes in Europe. This principle states that decisions should only be taken at a European level on matters that are truly European and where decisions at a Community level would be more effective. National and local governments should thus retain responsibility for those decisions that can be dealt with at their level. The principle of subsidiarity is officially adhered to by the Commission, but, in commonsense terms, it may seem difficult to reconcile with the Delors statement that 80 per cent of economic and social legislation may in the future be decided at the European level.

The concept of subsidiarity was invoked by Catholic social policy in the 1930s and was used by the Catholic church to defend its interests and to prevent state intervention. The term then re-emerged in the 1980s, prompted by national governments who feared that the powers of the Community were growing too fast.[27] The Commission has increasingly used the principle of subsidiarity in an attempt to offset these fears. In certain instances however, the Commission appears neatly to turn the subsidiarity principle on its head, by using it to justify action at the European level when it sees no action being taken at the local or national level.

The use of the concept of subsidiarity by the Commission has also grown in response to pressure from the German Lander (the German regional authorities) who have exclusive competence in certain areas under the German constitution, and who are concerned that Community legislation might interfere with those powers.[28] The principle of subsidiarity thus has important implications for the development of regional power within Europe. The Commission now sometimes refers to the Europe of the future as a 'Europe of the Regions', with direct political access from the regions to the EC, in parallel with national governments. The subsidiarity debate is particularly significant for Scotland, Wales and Northern Ireland, although England, with its lack of regional structure, would clearly be at a disadvantage.

A Wider Europe

It is important to realise that the future of the EC will also be dependent on what is happening in the wider Europe. Austria, Turkey, Cyprus and Malta have already applied to become members. Discussions have been taking place with the European Free Trade Association (EFTA) about the creation of a wider economic space with limited trade agreements between EC and EFTA countries. However, such discussions have not met with success as the members of EFTA would prefer to apply for full membership of the EC, rather than to adopt what they see as the partial solution of limited trade agreements.

The changes in Eastern Europe have already led to East Germany joining the Community as part of a united Germany. In other East European countries there will be trading opportunities and a wish to call on the experience of the countries of the Community as they struggle towards establishing or re-establishing democratic practices and institutions. The Community's PHARE programme is already making large allocations of money to Eastern Europe governments to assist in the restructuring of their economies. Some of these countries, for example Hungary, have indicated their desire to become members of the Community in the long term. For the present the Community is not considering any enlargement until the single European market programme is complete, but it is clear that a substantial increase in the number of member states would radically affect the future shape and political role of the Community.

As well as considering relationships with other countries in Europe, the Community has to look at the effects of its policies on the developing world. A report from the Overseas Development Institute has attempted to assess the costs of 1992 on developing countries.[29] There may be gains for some developing countries from increased demand for primary goods, and from an increase in prices as a result of the increased demand. However, there could also be negative effects on manufacturing industry in some developing countries, which could suffer if there is increased protectionism and purchasing of European goods. The move to free trade within EC boundaries could lead to an increase in trading activities and so to a boost for manufacturing in developing countries, but there is also the danger that the Community will pass on the burden of adjustment to the developing countries in the form of protectionism.

CONCLUSION

The SEA and 1992 primarily represent an economic programme with a specific date for implementing a range of measures aimed at eliminating all trading barriers between the 12 EC countries. However, it is important not to be mesmerised by the concept of a single date and a single programme. There is a real sense in which 1992 is a symbol for a much wider concept of social and political integration that ultimately could lead to a United States of Europe, a federation which would have far-reaching implications. Although this is the general direction in which developments are moving, it is still of course impossible to predict the final outcome.

27

Many of the concerns of voluntary and community organisations in the UK do not lie within the competence or the interest of the Community at present, or in the foreseeable future. On the other hand, it is likely that the changes in European context and policy will have *some* impact on *all* voluntary and community organisations, and that it will be central to the concerns of some of them. No organisation can afford to ignore what is happening within the EC. The decisions taken about its future will change the political and economic context for all our activities.

REFERENCES

---

1   Palmer, J. (1989) *1992 and Beyond.* Commission of the European Communities; Lodge, J. (ed.) *The European Community and the Challenge of the Future*, Pinter.

2   Grahl, J. and Teague, P. (1990) *1992 The Big Market: The Future of the European Community*, Lawrence and Wishart.

3   Speech to European Parliament June 1988, quoted in Palmer, in Lodge, *The European Community and the Challenge of the Future.*

4   Marquand, D. in *The Guardian*, 1 February, 1991.

5   Quoted in *The Guardian*, 12 March, 1991.

6   CEC (1987) *Treaties establishing the European Communities* (abridged edition). Office for Official Publications of the European Communities.

7   Pinder, J. (1989) 'The Single Market: A Step Towards European Union', in Lodge, *The European Community and the Challenge of the Future.*

8   CEC (1985) *European Commission White Paper on the Measures Necessary for the Completion of the Community's Internal Market.* COM (85) 310 final.

9   CEC *Treaties Establishing the European Communities.*

10 Harmonisation is the process of fixing common laws and standards for all member states. It can be contrasted with 'approximation' - the process of reaching agreement on measures which make the national laws in the various member states more similar, but not identical. Definitions from Crampton, S. (1990) *1992 Eurospeak Explained*, Rosters.

11 Cecchini, P. (1988) *The European Challenge 1992 The Benefits of a Single Market*, Wildwood House.

12 Grahl and Teague, *1992 The Big Market.*

13   *The Guardian*, 5 February, 1991.

14   Madelin, quoted in Teague, P. (1989) *The European Community: The Social Dimension. Labour Market Policies for 1992*, Cranfield School of Management, Monograph 4 p112.

15   Delors, J. (1988) *Europe 1992: The Social Dimension*. Address to Trade Union Congress September 1988; CEC (1988) *Social Dimension of the Internal Market*, Commission Working Paper, SEC(88) final.

16   CEC (1990) *Social Dimension 1992: The Community Worker's Charter and Supplementary Action Programme*. Background report. ISEC/B18/90.

17   Quote from Andre Kirchberger of Commissioner Papandreou's cabinet. From an article on Implementing the Social Charter in *The European Citizen*, 1 June 1990.

18   Department of Trade and Industry (1990) *The Single Market: The Facts*. Fact sheet 34 DTI.

19   Information on observatories was provided by Diana Robbins.

20   Palmer, J. (1991) 'EC Federalists Are Not What They Seem'. *The Guardian*, 19 June.

21   *The Guardian*, 1 July 1991.

22   Davison, A. and Seary, B. (1990) *Grants from Europe*, Bedford Square Press.

23   Davison, and Seary, *Grants from Europe*.

24   CEC (1990) *Europe Our Future: The Institutions of the European Community*. European File 16/89, CEC and EP.

25   Lodge, *The European Community and the Challenge of the Future*.

26   Bogdanor, V. (1989) 'Direct Elections, Representative Democracy and European Integration', *Electoral Studies*, 83 pp205-216.

27   Spiker, P. (1991) 'The Principle of Subsidiarity and the Social Policy of the European Community'. *Journal of European Social Policy*. 1:1 pp3-14.

28   Wilke, M. and Wallace, H. (1990) *Subsidiarity: Approaches to Power Sharing in the European Community* Royal Institute of International Affairs Discussion Paper 27; Norton, A. (1991) Western European Local Government in Comparative Perspective in Batley, R. and Stoker, G. (eds.) *Local Government in Europe: Trends and Developments*, Macmillan Education.

29   Davenport, M. and Page, S. (1991) *Europe: 1992 and the Developing World*, Overseas Development Institute.

2

The Voluntary and Community Sectors and Europe: Setting the Scene

INTRODUCTION

What will the new Europe mean for voluntary and community organisations? How will their day-to-day work be affected by new European legislation, and how will economic changes affect the communities in which voluntary and community organisations work? This chapter gives an introduction to some of the impacts that a more integrated and competitive Europe may have on the voluntary and community sectors, and explores how they are currently perceived within Europe. First, however, it describes the policy context in which voluntary and community organisations are operating in the UK. The European dimension is just one, albeit extremely important, of the many challenges facing the UK voluntary and community sectors in the 1990s, and these challenges will inevitably place competing demands upon organisations.

THE UK CONTEXT

The UK voluntary sector has been described as being 'on the brink of massive change'.[1] In the early 1990s voluntary organisations find themselves centre-stage in the most significant restructuring of the welfare state since its inception. As Kramer writes:

31

It was not long ago that the major concern of the voluntary sector in Britain was about its declining role; now, in contrast, there is anxiety because it may face an expanding role in the 1990s due to major changes in the policy context and the emergence of a new, Conservative paradigm of the British welfare state.[2]

As part of its programme to limit state expenditure and involvement in the provision of welfare, and to reduce the role of local authorities, central government has required the contracting-out of many local authority functions, and has offered voluntary organisations a seductive opportunity to expand their role in service-provision.[3] The significance of this change for voluntary organisations is most apparent in the field of community care. Local and health authorities are to become purchasers rather than providers of care, and will increasingly be contracting non-statutory organisations (private and voluntary) to provide community care on the state's behalf. Community care is not the only area in which a greater role has been envisaged for voluntary organisations. The 1989 Children Act also placed emphasis on local authorities developing partnerships with voluntary organisations in child care and child protection services.[4]

These changes in welfare provision are occurring at the same time as a marked increase in social needs. There are, for example, growing numbers of elderly people,[5] an increase in the number of homeless people,[6] and more people seeking advice on welfare and financial problems than ever before.[7]

The paradox for voluntary organisations is that as they face the challenges of tendering and sub-contracting and providing for increasing social needs, many are simultaneously suffering a severe and sometimes fatal financial crisis. NCVO has argued:

> It is difficult to find anywhere in England and Wales where the voluntary sector is expanding; at best, activity is at a standstill, at worst, jobs, services and whole community organisations have been lost ... as millions of pounds are slashed from grants budgets.[8]

Charge-capping has been the major cause of cuts in grant aid, forcing some local authorities to drastically cut their support to voluntary and community organisations. Furthermore, there are increasing concerns that the shift towards contract-funding will selectively discriminate in favour of the larger service-providing voluntary organisations, and that funding for advocacy, advice and information, and for smaller community organisations may become more restricted. Chanan suggests that: 'all political parties want the voluntary sector to do more, yet current policies are leading to the destruction of large parts of it'.[9]

THE EFFECTS OF THE SINGLE EUROPEAN MARKET

Part Two of this report identifies key policy issues and population groups addressed by the voluntary and community sectors, and explores specific impacts in each of these areas. In this preliminary chapter some of the likely effects of 1992 are identified according to the various functions of voluntary and community organisations. The typology of functions used is one suggested by Brenton.[10] Although based on the voluntary sector of the mid-1980s rather than the rapidly changing pattern of the 1990s, this typology still offers a useful classification of many of the functions of voluntary and community organisations:

- the service-providing function;

- the pressure-group function;

- the resource and co-ordinating function;

- the self-help and mutual-aid function.

A further function which can be added to this list is that of fund raising.

As Brenton suggests, these functional categories should be seen as ideal types, rather than as precise descriptions. In reality, organisations may conduct a range of activities, but it is often still possible to pinpoint some major defining function in an organisation.

Implications for the Service-Providing Function

This function typifies voluntary organisations which supply a direct service to people, in kind or in the form of information, advice, or support. It would include, for example, Citizens Advice Bureaux as well as Barnardo's, the Spastics Society and some local Age Concern groups.

A major effect of a more competitive and integrated European market for such organisations will be changes in the pattern of needs which they attempt to address. Part Two of this report describes how 1992 could result in increased unemployment in some regions, greater numbers of people living in poverty, and a reduction in social rights for migrants and refugees in Europe. Voluntary and community organisations will be at the front-line of these changing patterns of social needs. Organisations involved with advice-giving will need to equip themselves with new information on rights

33

within the EC - the rights of Europeans to work in different countries, and the rights of migrants working in the EC, for example. The European Commission's Citizen's Advisory Service has published a series of fact-sheets 'to inform people of their rights as citizens in the context of the creation of the Single Market within the EC by 1992'.[11] Advice agencies will need to familiarise themselves with the contents of such material.

A second effect of a single European market for service-providing voluntary organisations is likely to be increasing competition for public contracts. A central plank of the 1992 project has been the exposure of government procurement to more open competitive tendering across frontiers. State purchasing is a vast market - it has been estimated to amount to 15 per cent of the collective gross domestic product of the 12 member states, and to date only a small part of this market has been open to tender. European directives on public procurement will now mean the opening up of public sector contracts to greater competition within the EC, so that national, regional and local authorities will be legally obliged to advertise invitations to tender for service contracts throughout Europe. Examples of relevant service contracts for voluntary organisations include provision of residential care for elderly people, child care and waste recycling. The directives will apply to any contract worth more than 200,000 ECUs (about £140,000).[12]

Therefore, 1992 will mean that some of the largest voluntary organisations will have the chance to tender for service contracts not only in their own countries but also in other member states. There may also be increasing competition from agencies in other member states for contracts in the UK. NCVO has suggested that, taken together with the British government's own policy on contracting out of welfare services, the public procurement directives will be 'a significant boost to competition in many of the markets in which voluntary organisations are active'.[13] It is impossible to predict how much competition will develop, but it is salutory to note that the leading German welfare organisations have set up offices in Brussels, in response to 'the danger' of other welfare organisations competing with them for the provision of social services in Germany.[14]

Thirdly, 1992 is likely to result in changes in VAT relief for charities in the UK. Many voluntary organisations receive fiscal benefits under UK tax law because of their charitable status. Specifically, zero-rating VAT relief is given to charities in respect of certain goods and services they buy. As part of the 1992 programme, the Commission proposes to approximate VAT throughout the EC. The concern of the Charity Commission and the Charity Tax Reform Group, representing the views of many UK charities, has been that European legislation may result in charities losing these fiscal benefits. Oxfam, for example, has estimated that abolishing the zero-rating could cost it £5.75 million a year. At the final meeting of the European Finance Ministers under the Luxembourg Presidency in June 1991, the Council agreed that all zero rates in existence on 1 January 1991 could continue at least until 1996. This means that the threat of significantly increased VAT bills (potentially an extra £500 million pa) facing UK charities has for the time being been lifted. In order to change this arrangement, the Council of Ministers would have to vote unanimously for its abolition. This effectively means that as long as the UK government can be persuaded to keep zero-rates for charities, it is unlikely that UK charities will lose these benefits.[15]

There are many other legal and technical changes as a result of 1992 that could affect voluntary and community organisations involved in some form of service activity. For example:

- The Commission's proposals to extend the rights and protections of full-time workers to part-time and temporary workers would affect the employment conditions of many employees of voluntary and community organisations, although this directive is currently being blocked, primarily by the British government (Chapter 6).

- One of the new health and safety directives to come into force on 1 January 1993 will require all employers to introduce certain safety requirements for VDU operators, and to identify workers' rights to training and consultation on the introduction of VDUs (Chapter 6).

- In January 1991, the first general system for the mutual recognition of professional and vocational qualifications came into force. This means that all professional qualifications involving three or more years of study beyond secondary level should be recognised throughout the EC, although precise equivalents have not yet been agreed in every area. It is impossible at this stage to predict the effects of the mutual recognition provisions on voluntary organisations, although it is thought that any mass movements of professional labour is unlikely to occur.[16]

- The EC directive on driver licences could dramatically affect community transport provision in the UK, requiring voluntary organisations to spend substantial sums of money on training and testing minibus and playbus drivers.[17]

Implications for the Pressure-Group Function

The pressure-group function:

> implies the marshalling of information and argument around some specific cause or group interest and the application of this in some public arena through direct action, campaigning, lobbying and advocacy in order to achieve a desired change.[18]

35

Examples of this type of organisation are the Child Poverty Action Group, Friends of the Earth, Liberty (previously the National Council for Civil Liberties) and the Disability Alliance. The shift away from national towards European decision and policy-making is already having, and will continue to have, major implications for the work of such organisations.

Europe is increasingly becoming an important new campaigning space. The European institutions present new opportunities for lobbying and pressure-group activities, a challenge that the commercial sector has grasped to its advantage for some time, and one that many in the voluntary and community sectors are now beginning to explore. Some argue that the current imbalance between economic and social policy in the EC has been exacerbated by a corresponding imbalance to date in the interest groups lobbying the European institutions. Voluntary organisations comprise only about one per cent of the total of 500 organisations and 3,000 lobbyists estimated to be centred around the EC.[19] A more integrated and competitive Europe will require that voluntary and community organisations quickly equip themselves with new skills and knowledge, additional resources, and new ways of developing and sharing pressure-group activities, often on a cross-national basis (see European networks below). Hoskyns suggests that, to date, lobbying in Brussels has been: 'an elitist affair, with lobbyists seeking autonomy rather than accountability. But transnational politics of a genuinely popular kind is desperately needed if the hold of the techno-bureaucrats and business elites is to be challenged in Brussels'.[20]

Implications for the Resource and Co-ordinating Function

A prime purpose of some voluntary and community organisations is to service other organisations, or to act as a central catalyst or repository of expertise, information and research - in other words, to provide a resource and co-ordination function. For example, the two organisations sponsoring this report, NCVO and CDF, fall into this category, as do The Volunteer Centre and the National Alliance of Women's Organisations. Such organisations will increasingly find their constituencies identifying a need for detailed policy analysis of European developments. This report represents one attempt to assist organisations in this process.

A further implication of greater European integration for such organisations is the impetus it is giving to the development of cross-national networks. It is becoming clear that in addition to their vertical relationships

SOME GENERALIST EUROPEAN NETWORKS OF INTEREST TO THE VOLUNTARY SECTOR

Comité Européen des Associations d'Intérêt Général (CEDAG) aims to be the European Council for Voluntary Organisations and acts as a resource for co-ordination and information exchange. CEDAG can be contacted through Groupement National Associatif pour l'Économie Sociale, 18 rue de Varenne, 75007 Paris, France.

Euro-Citizen-Action-Service (ECAS) is an information and advocacy service, based in Brussels, which aims to strengthen the voice of voluntary organisations within the EC. It produces a regular magazine (*The European Citizen*), holds seminars on the EC decision-making process and provides advice to individual organisations on developing a European strategy, identifying the right contacts and forming European partnerships with similar bodies in other EC countries. ECAS works mainly in the areas of citizens' rights, health, social welfare and culture. It can be contacted at 98 rue du Trône, B-1050 Brussels.

European Social Action Network (ESAN) is an initiative established by a number of non-governmental social welfare and social development agencies within the EC. Its objectives are to create awareness of social problems within the EC, to stimulate and influence policy making for social welfare and social development, and to monitor social issues within the wider international context. A small staff team is establishing a documentation, advice and information service for members in Brussels. ESAN can be contacted at 98 rue du Trône, B-1050 Brussels.

The Combined European Bureau For Social Development brings together agencies from nine countries to promote community and social development throughout Europe. It organises conferences, training events and exchange programmes in several European countries. The European Bureau for Social Development can be contacted at PO Box 61677, 2506 AD The Hague, The Netherlands.

European Foundation Centre (EFC) acts as a forum and networking centre for grant giving bodies, not only in Europe but also in the United States and Japan. It monitors EC policy that might affect grant-giving bodies. It holds training programmes and seminars and has a particular concern with developments in Central and Eastern Europe. The Centre is based at 51 rue de la Concorde, 1050 Brussels.

International Council On Social Welfare (ICSW) is a world organisation, founded in 1929, which promotes social development. Its European region, working through a network of national committees, enables international contacts and policy discussions. Its priority, at present, is work on issues of poverty in Europe, on which it is in contact with EC and Council of Europe institutions. ICSW-Europe Region can be contacted through Dirk Jarre, President of the European Region of ICSW, AM Stockborn, 1-3, D-6000 Frankfurt/Main 50, Federal Republic of Germany.

International Federation of Settlements and Neighbourhood Centres European Network (IFS). The main focus of this network is in the field of community development, but IFS recognises that it is unhelpful to be restrictive about the contacts in a network of this kind and welcomes anyone with an interest in the social aspects of 1992. Special emphasis is currently given to multicultural work and community media projects. The IFS European Network can be contacted through Christian Kunz, c/o Birmingham Settlement, 318 Summer Lane, Birmingham B19 3RL.

Volunteurope is a network of organisations from EC countries who are concerned with the use of volunteers. Volunteurope can be contacted through Mrs Elisabeth Hoodless, President, Volunteurope, c/o Community Service Volunteers, 237 Pentonville Road, London N1 9UJ.

Information in this box was supplied by NCVO, Brian Harvey and ECAS.

with member states and regional authorities, the Commission is also cultivating horizontal relationships with cross-national networks of organisations, including voluntary and community sector networks (discussed further in Chapter 10). Harvey[21] notes that about 60 networks of voluntary organisations concerned with social policy have now been established in the EC and that they are proliferating. Co-ordinating bodies will increasingly be faced with the task of facilitating this process of networking, requiring new skills in building links and mobilising action between grassroots groups and issues in quite different political, economic and social cultures. Voluntary and community organisations have considerable experience in building coalitions and networks at the local and national levels. The challenge will now be to engage in similar activities across Europe.

Part Two of this report describes a number of the issue-specific European networks in which UK voluntary and community organisations are participating.[22] A selection of more general European networks and resource agencies are described in Box E (pages 37-8).

Implications for the Self-Help and Mutual-Aid Function

Organisations whose primary function is self-help or mutual aid (such as CRUSE for widows, and a range of other women's self-help groups) may find it hard to immediately see the relevance of 1992 to their particular common need or interest. The single European market is unlikely, in either the short- or long-term, to impinge directly on the everyday activities of, for example, an anorexia self-help group. However, for some groups 1992 could mean that a raised profile is given to their interests and concerns. For example, cancer self-help groups have been involved in the Europe against Cancer programme (page 118), and many women's groups have welcomed the attention the EC has given to a range of equal opportunities issues, particularly at a time when they have such low priority at the national political level (Chapter 6).

The self-help function of organisations can be extended to include self-governing community groups involved with local self-development, such as tenants' groups and other grassroots organisations. As with individual self-help groups, it may be hard for such groups to see any immediate relevance of 1992 to their own communities. However, a central argument of this report 1992 is likely to exacerbate the processes and consequences of industrial restructuring experienced in the UK throughout the 1970s and 1980s, leaving many communities with higher levels of job-loss, unemployment, and greater needs for local self-development activities. Voluntary and community organisations often find that they are in the forefront of efforts to alleviate or transform this kind of longer-term socio-economic impact. These implications are discussed in detail in Chapter 3.

Implications for the fund-raising function

Europe will increasingly offer some organisations new possibilities for raising funds, as more EC programmes of relevance to voluntary and community organisations are announced by the Commission.[23] However, a note of caution is needed: groups that have obtained funds have often found that alongside the advantage of securing additional monies have come a number of problems. These have required an appreciation of the EC not just as a straightforward source of money, but rather as a complex new bureaucracy and political mechanism.

The year 1992 is almost certain to have an effect on corporate giving to voluntary organisations. It may be that as a result of economic restructuring some 'cosy' relationships between local funders and voluntary organisations are disturbed.[24]   At a national level, companies such as BP and IBM may be considering shifting their UK-based community affairs departments to Europe, and making their community funds available to organisations throughout Europe.   A directory of company-giving in Europe is being published by the Directory of Social Change.[25]   It is also likely that independent trusts and foundations will have new demands on their resources, and the European Foundation Centre has been established in Brussels as a networking service centre for grant-giving concerns (Box E). Finally, EC legislation may have implications for fundraising from the public. For example, some charities, including Age Concern and the RSPCA, are concerned that the proposed European data protection law - aimed at protecting consumers from junk mail - could outlaw the computerised lists that allow them to target fundraising appeals.[26]   A group called CHANGE (Charities and Non-Profit Groups in Europe) has been formed to represent the interests of charity fundraising in Europe.[27]

THE VOLUNTARY AND COMMUNITY SECTORS AND THE EUROPEAN INSTITUTIONS

Greater European integration will mean that voluntary and community organisations will increasingly want to learn more about their counterparts in other member states, and appreciate the diversity of the voluntary or 'non-governmental' sector across Europe.   It is not within the remit of this report to give a detailed description of the voluntary and community sectors in different member states, but the reader is referred to Appendix D, where Robbins provides a useful summary of available data about the scale, scope and structure of the social welfare voluntary sector in each of the 12 European countries.[28]   In addition, a research study at the University of Kent is currently conducting a comparative analysis of the non-profit sector in Europe, the United States and Japan, focusing on the legal structure of this sector, its historical development, and key policy issues.[29]

This section focuses therefore on how the EC's view of voluntary organisations appears to be developing. What overall status do voluntary and community organisations have within the institutions of Europe?   It is possible to explore this question at both a practical, and a legal and technical level.   At a *practical* level, there are some indications that the Commission and European Parliament are taking the voluntary sector seriously and wish to develop dialogue with its representatives.   Over the last few years the

Commission has not only funded, but has actively sought the development of, a number of the cross-national networks of voluntary organisations referred to above. Furthermore, Harvey notes that in October 1990 the European Parliament voted two million ECUs (about £1.4 million) to fund new networks, and suggests that this is a clear indication of the value the European Parliament places on the work of voluntary organisations in agenda-setting and in providing ideas and information for social initiatives.[30]

Why is the Commission interested in seeking the views of voluntary organisations and encouraging its participation in the European process? Harvey suggests:

> The Commission's precise reasons for funding these networks and associations have never been clarified, beyond generalized statements about seeking convergence in social policies: one may speculate that it is simpler for the Commission to deal with a single source of international opinion on a particular social issue or sector than twelve national organizations at a time. Voluntary organizations may also be in a position to provide the Commission with information and research on social developments that is a valuable complement - or even a counter - to that provided by national governments. This information may in turn fuel the ambitious social agendas of individual sections of the Commission, or its President. For their part, hardened members of some of the networks suspect that funding network activity is, in the overall scheme of things, an inexpensive method of expressing social concern and 'putting a human face' on 1992.[31]

Other commentators have suggested that an important reason why the EC is initiating links with voluntary organisations is that they provide additional channels for stimulating and legitimising EC activity in member states even when national governments may be reluctant. This certainly seems to have been one of the effects in the UK of the European programmes to combat poverty. The second of these programmes (which ran from 1985-1989) depended heavily on voluntary sector involvement, at a time when the British government was denying the existence of poverty and therefore resisting any responsibility for tackling it.

In exploring the developing relationship between voluntary organisations and the European institutions, it is important to consider the changing relationships between the national and local state and the voluntary and community sectors. Many of the European countries are moving towards a mixed economy of welfare, in which service-providing organisations will tend to become financially dependent upon contracts from the state, and/or may move into joint ventures with the private sector. A consequence is likely to be a blurring of the boundaries between the voluntary and the public sectors. This trend carries with it the dangers of virtual incorporation by the

41

state, or of merging into the commercial values of the private sector, with a corresponding loss of ability to act independently. The crucial question is what effect such developments will have on the relationships currently being forged between voluntary organisations and Europe.

In exploring the status of voluntary and community organisations in Europe at the *legal* and *technical* level, the picture becomes even more complex. The European institutions regard many charities and voluntary organisations as falling within the category of 'associations', a term which has a legal meaning throughout most of Europe, similar to the way in which the term 'charity' or 'company limited by guarantee' has a particular legal status in the UK. Associations, along with the rather dissimilar co-operatives, mutual credit and mutual insurance organisations, are regarded as part of *l'économie sociale* - a French concept, now adopted by the Commission.[32] The common feature of organisations within *l'économie sociale* is that they engage in economic activity, not with a view to making profits for distribution, but for the benefit of the community at large, and more particularly of their members.[33] Even though many of the voluntary sector's relationships with the Commission are through Directorate General V (the division responsible for social affairs), Directorate General XXIII, which is responsible for *l'économie sociale*, is formally the division within which voluntary and community organisations are considered to fall (Appendix C).

The Commission's deliberations about *l'économie sociale* represent a major step in getting voluntary organisations on to the EC agenda.[34] Many voluntary organisations in the UK are increasingly engaged in forms of economic activity - selling goods through charity shops, or providing a service that clients may pay for in part or in full, and so in this sense the Commission's thinking has a certain logic to it. Nevertheless, there is much resistance among those representing the interests of charities in the UK to the Commission's attempt to line up *l'économie sociale* with the UK voluntary sector. A number of points have been raised in opposition. First, it is suggested that the bodies banded together within *l'économie sociale* do not form any coherent set of organisations:

> The principal institutions of *l'économie sociale* - the co-operatives, for example, and the mutual financial institutions - are engaged in commercial activity because that is their essential purpose; and they seek the interest of their members because that is what they are in business to seek. Charities, however, are never engaged in commercial activity for its own sake... No more may charities seek the interest of their members; their interests always have to be altruistic.[35]

It is therefore suggested that because of their lack of common philosophy, it is misleading to treat UK charities as of similar character to the other constituents of l'économie sociale. Second, it is argued, that the inclusion of

UK voluntary organisations within l'économie sociale may eventually threaten the fiscal privileges enjoyed by registered charities (depending upon the final interpretation of particular articles within the Treaty of Rome) because charities may find themselves subject to European legislation rather than national charity law.[36]

CONCLUSION

This chapter has indicated a wide range of possible impacts of the single European market for the voluntary and community sectors. It has also discussed some of the opportunities and dangers presented by 1992 and explored the ways in which the European institutions are developing relationships with voluntary and community organisations. The importance of considering the changes occurring at a *European* level within the context of *national* policy changes has been stressed, and in this context the competing demands and challenges facing voluntary organisations in the 1990s were identified.

REFERENCES

1   Heginbotham, C. (1990) *Return to the Community*, Bedfor d Square Press.

2   Kramer, R. (1991) 'Change and Continuity in UK Voluntary Organisations, 1976 to 1988', *Voluntas*, 12 pp33-60.

3   Taylor, M. (1990) *New Times, New Challenges: Voluntary Organisations Facing 1990.* NCVO; Gutch, R., Kunz, C. and Spencer, K. (1990) *Partners or Agents? Local Government and the Voluntary Sector - Changing Relationships in the 1990s*, NCVO.

4   NCVO (1991) *A Contracting Sector? The Impact of the Poll Tax and Other Funding Changes on the Voluntary Sector*, NCVO.

5   Central Statistical Office (1991), *Social Trends*, 21 HMSO.

6   Central Statistical Office, *Social Trends.*

7   Advice Services Alliance (1991) *Government Action Requested to Protect Advice Services From Financial Crisis.* Press Release, 8 March, 1991.

8   NCVO, *A Contracting Sector?*

9   Chanan, G. (1991) *Taken for Granted: Community Activity and the Crisis of the Voluntary Sector*. A response to the Labour Party consultative document 'Labour and the Voluntary Sector'. Community Development Foundation.

10   Brenton, M. (1985) *The Voluntary Sector in British Social Services*. Longman.

11   These leaflets are available from the Commission of the European Communities, Citizen's Europe Advisory Service, 8 Storey's Gate, London SW1P 3AT.

12   Perri 6, (1991) *Impacts of European Union: Issues for NCVO Policy, Research and Legal Action.* NCVO.

13   Perri 6, *Impacts of European Union.*

14   Harvey, B. (1991a) *Pressure Groups and Policy Making in the European Communities*, Paper presented to Nuffield College, Oxford, European Studies Centre, 17-19 May, 1991.

15   Information supplied by Nigel Tarling, International Officer at NCVO, from *Euronews*, September 1991, Issue 6. For further information on the implications of VAT changes for charities, contact NCVO, or the Charities Tax Reform Group, 9 Old Queen Street, Westminster, London SW1H 9JA.

16   Perri 6, *Impacts of European Union.*

17   See article in *Euromonitor* September, 1990. Euromonitor is a regular bulletin produced by the Directory of Social Change, Radius Works, Back Lane, London NW3 1HL.

18   Brenton, *The Voluntary Sector* in British Social Services.

19   Harvey, *Pressure Groups and Policy Making in the European Communities.*

20   Hoskyns, (1991) The European Women's Lobby *Feminist Review*, Autumn (forthcoming)

21   Personal communication, June, 1991.

22   For further information on European networks and their relevance to voluntary and community organisations, see Harvey, B. (1992) *Networking in Europe: A Guide to European Voluntary Organisations*, NCVO Publications.

23   For details of grants available from Europe, see Davison, A. and Seary, B. (1990) *Grants From Europe*, Sixth Edition. Bedford Square Press.

24 See Perri 6, *Impacts of European Union*.

25 Dabson, B. (1991) *Company Giving in Europe*. Directory of Social Change (forthcoming).

26 For further information on the EC draft directive on data protection see *Euronews*, 5 May 1991.

27 CHANGE can be contacted through Gavin Grant, CHANGE, c/o ICFM, Market Towers, 1 Nine Elms Lane, London SW8 5NQ.

28 Appendix D is taken from Robbins, D. (1991) 'Voluntary Organisations and the Social State in the European Community', *Voluntas*, 1, 2 pp98-128.

29 For further details of this study, contact Martin Knapp, PSSRU, University of Kent at Canterbury, Canterbury, Kent CT2 7NF.

30 Harvey, B. (1991b) 'European networks of Voluntary Organisations - a new development?' *Critical Public Health*, 1 pp30-35

31 Harvey, *Pressure Groups and Policy Making in the European Communities*.

32 CEC, (1989) *Business in the 'Économie Sociale' sector* Commission document. SEC (89) 2187 of 18 December 89

33 Kidd, H. (1990) *A Further Look at 1992*. Directory of Social Change.

34 See article on *'The Économie Sociale'* and The Single Europe in *Euromonitor*, May 1990.

35 Kidd, *A Further Look at 1992*.

36 For further discussion of this point, see Kidd, *A Further Look at 1992*.

PART TWO

3

Economic Change, Employment and Training

INTRODUCTION

What effect will the single European market have on local economies, the number and type of jobs available, and the patterns of employment and unemployment throughout Europe? This chapter addresses these questions by looking at current economic and employment trends in Europe, and discussing the possible effects of 1992 on industry, jobs, training, and the labour market. The activities of the Commission in the area of employment and training are identified, and the role of the voluntary and community sectors in responding to the employment opportunities and dangers of 1992 are examined. Labour market issues of particular relevance to women are explored in more detail in Chapter 6 and some of the trends identified are also pertinent to the male workforce.

Current employment trends

In 1989 there were approximately 133 million people in employment in the EC - around half the total population. This figure has been increasing steadily since 1965, mainly due to the increases in the population of working age as the post-war baby-boom filters through into the labour market. Between 1985 and 1988 there was a net addition of 4.8 million jobs, primarily filled by more young people and women coming into the labour market. Unemployment fell by only 1.1 million during this period (from 14.9 to 13.8 million), and the proportion of unemployed people who had been out of work for more than a year stayed constant at just over 50 per cent (7.5 million). There was a further fall in unemployment of about one million in 1989 and this trend continued into 1990.[1] However, the recession of late 1990 and 1991 reversed the trend, with unemployment figures starting to rise sharply again by mid-1991.

Within the total workforce there are continuing changes in the structure of employment. Nearly all the new jobs that have been created are in service activities. Employment in service activities increased in all the member states but was particularly marked in the UK. By contrast, very few extra jobs were created in manufacturing industry, and the number of jobs in agriculture has continued to decline.

THE EFFECTS OF THE SINGLE EUROPEAN MARKET

It is difficult of course to distinguish the effects of 1992 from the effects of other more general and global economic changes. According to Cecchini[2] (page 11), a more integrated European market could result in increases in overall employment ranging from a minimum of 1.8 million to a maximum of 5.7 million, depending on accompanying macro-economic measures which may be taken by various governments. However, the margin of accuracy of these figures is estimated at plus or minus 30 per cent. Others have argued that this job creation will not happen just because of the single market, but will largely be dependent upon general growth within the economies of member states,[3] and that the single market will simply highlight and support trends already in operation.

There are also major uncertainties about the distribution of the economic and employment benefits and costs of 1992 between different sectors, countries, regions and localities. In particular, the creation of a more integrated and more competitive European market seems likely to set in motion a further wave of economic and industrial restructuring which could have major impacts on many regions and local economies in terms of increased job loss and unemployment.

Vulnerable Industries

One of the declared purposes of the single market is to deliver a 'supply-side shock' to the European economic system. The diagnosis is that European-based industries are not lean and hungry enough to be competitive with Japanese and American industries in global or European markets. It is argued that one of the main symptoms of the sluggishness in the European

TABLE 2

LIST OF THE 40 SENSITIVE INDUSTRIES

Office and data processing machinery
Telecommunications
Medical and surgical equipment
Pharmaceutical product
Boilermaking
Loco motives, tramways
Champagnes, sparkling wines
Brewing and malting
Soft drinks
Insulated wires and cables
Electrical machinery
Shipbuilding
Spaghetti, macaroni, etc
Cocoa, chocolate and sugar confectionary
Glass and glassware
Ceramic goods
Basic industrial chemicals
Other chemical products mainly for industrial and agricultural purposes
Machine-tools for working metal
Textile machinery
Machinery for food, chemical and related industry
Plant for mines, iron and steel industy
Transmission equipment for motive power
Other machihnery for specific branches
Radio and television
Electric appliances
Electric lamps and other electric lighting
Motor vehicles
Aerospace equipment
Wool industry
Cotton industry
Carpets
Footwear
Clothing
Household textiles
Rubber products
Jewellery
Photographic and cinematographic laboratories
Toys and sports goods

Source: Buignes, P. & Ilzkovitz, F. (1988) *The Sectoral Impact of the Internal Market*, DG II/33S/88 Brussels: CEC

economy is over-production or over-capacity in too many industrial sectors. The removal of various barriers to free trade, for example, protectionist public purchasing is seen as one way of exposing firms to sharper competition and stimulating restructuring through mergers, takeovers, joint ventures and plant closures.[4]

European Commission studies have identified 40 sectors of industry which are likely to be particularly sensitive to the changes that will occur in creating a single European market[5] (Table 2). Examples of vulnerable industries highlighted by these studies include:

- **Boilermaking,** where the EC currently has 12 producers, compared with only six in the United States for a market of a similar size: Cecchini's estimate is that the opening up of a single European market would eliminate some of this over-production and reduce the sector to no more than four firms in Europe during the 1990s, and reduce costs by about 20 per cent.

- **Turbine generators,** where there are currently 10 producers in Europe, compared with only two in the United States.

- **Telephone exchange equipment,** where there are 11 producers in Europe compared with four in the United States. The forecast in the Cecchini Report is that the single European market will reduce the number of European manufacturers to only two during 1990s.

Major changes are also occurring in European agricultural industries and farming. The intensification of competition as a result of 1992, and the removal or run down of European subsidies through the CAP, will together accelerate the restructuring of this sector which has experienced over-production for many years. For example, the European Commissioner for Agriculture and Rural Development, Mr Ray Macsharry, has spoken of:

the unavoidable adjustment of farming in Europe to market realities and the implications of this adjustment, not only for farmers and farm workers, but also for the rural economy in general. This adjustment accompanies the modernisation and intensification of production processes, the consequent reduction in the acreage used for agriculture and a sharp decline in the number of farmers and farm workers... Over the period 1965-85 the numbers working on the land fell by one half: it is estimated that by the end of the century between 6 million and 16 million hectares of farm land will be surplus to needs.[6]

These changes are also expected to have implications within Europen agribusiness. For example, there are currently 50 tractor manufacturers in Western Europe, competing for a market of about 200,000 tractor sales a year, compared with the United States where there are only four manufacturers for the same size of market.

It is interesting to note that the sectors identified as potentially vulnerable to restructuring are not restricted to the older, declining industries. They include newer and more modern industries such as data processing and lasers. Europe is not just facing another wave of de-industrialisation, but an even more fundamental restructuring of the whole pattern of ownership, control and location of industry, technology and employment.[7]

The net result of this economic restructuring may well be a 'zero-sum game'.[8] While the overall size of the cake may not increase substantially, the competition for shares of the cake could intensify considerably. In other words, industrial restructuring in a more competitive European market can only produce winners at the direct expense of losers. The chairman of Olivetti is quoted as saying that 'Despite all the singing and cheering, Europe's companies are marching off to war. A war that will have its dead and wounded...from which not everyone will come back a winner'.[9] Indeed, Sir John Harvey Jones, former chairman of ICI, has predicted that by the year 2000 more than half of Europe's factories could be closed and half its companies could disappear or be taken over.[10]

Changing Patterns of Ownership and Control

These waves of restructuring are likely to lead to a concentration and centralisation of control over industry and employment in Europe. The supply-side shock given by the 1992 programme will accelerate the process of internationalisation of companies. Decisions will tend to become concentrated in the hands of a smaller number of larger more powerful transnational firms aiming to reap the benefits of economies of scale, which can come from mass production for mass markets. Concentration of ownership and centralisation of control will mean new European, or even global, structures of industrial management and organisation, with more centralised headquarters and fewer production centres.[11] Where those headquarters are situated, and what happens to outlying branch plants, clearly has considerable consequences for investment and employment in those countries and regions in which they are situated.

The National and Regional Impacts

Assessments of the spatial effects of 1992 emphasise that the creation of a more competitive and integrated European market will widen existing disparities between the nations and regions of Europe. European Commission research for the Cecchini Report suggests that the single European market will have different impacts upon gross domestic product (GDP) and employment in different countries. Table 3 shows the UK and Italy suffering the sharpest initial loss of jobs in years one and two, and the lowest long-term gain in employment of all the member states. It also shows the UK as having the lowest gain in GDP over the period 1989-1995.

TABLE 3

CUMULATIVE IMPACT OF THE SINGLE MARKET ON GROSS DOMESTIC PRODUCT AND EMPLOYMENT

(Percentages on a cumulative basis)

		1989-1995					
		Yr 1	Yr 2	Yr 3	Yr 4	Yr 5	Yr 6
France:	GDP	1.1	2.0	2.9	3.7	4.4	5.1
	Employment	-0.3	0.0	0.3	0.7	1.21	1.6
Italy:	GDP	1.4	3.2	4.5	5.2	5.4	5.5
	Employment	-0.6	-0.2	0.3	0.7	1.1	1.4
UK:	GDP	0.8	2.4	3.3	3.6	3.8	4.0
	Employment	-0.6	-0.1	0.7	1.1	1.3	1.4
West Germany:	GDP	1.2	2.0	2.6	2.9	3.5	4.2
	Employment	-0.3	0.1	0.5	0.8	1.2	1.7
Europe-12	GDP	1.1	2.3	3.2	3.5	4.1	4.5
	Employment	-0.4	0.0	0.5	0.8	1.2	1.5

Source: Cecchini, P. (1988) *Research on the 'Costs of non-Europe'*. Basic Findings, CEC Brussels

Another study by Rajan concludes that the UK will bear the brunt of the job loss in the first year of the single market, with a loss of about 157,000 jobs. He argues that this is a 'best case' scenario because it does not take account of the accelerated pace of structural change since 1985 which will:

> either bring forward the timing of job losses or increase their scale: in all probability it will do both, the more so because it is already happening under the fierce operation of market forces that have their own momentum and logic. For the next five years or so, this momentum will accelerate. Under it the outcome will be simple and deterministic: the winner will take all.[12]

An even more pessimistic analysis by Neuberger, then economic adviser to the opposition spokesman on trade and industry, argues that the UK will experience a loss of about 120,000 jobs a year on average throughout the 1990s.[13] Neuberger's calculations show all the UK regions losing employment in the first half of the 1990s and only very small gains by 1998. The sharpest initial impact is predicted to be in the East Midlands and East Anglia, and over the whole period of the 1990s, the worst impact will be in the north west of England, Wales and Scotland.

These very pessimistic projections are confirmed by the Cambridge Regional Economic Review which anaylses the economic outlook for the regions and countries of the UK in the 1990s. The summary of their findings is that:

> In the North the prospects are bleak. For the Northern Region, the North West and Northern Ireland in the absence of any strengthening in regional policy, substantial falls in employment are projected... The major British conurbations are forecast to continue to lose jobs, although the picture is mixed with West Yorkshire experiencing a moderate decline, whilst Merseyside conurbation faces severe economic blight.[14]

The EC Commissioner responsible for regional policy, Bruce Millan, is officially quoted as saying he is 'frankly unhappy about the way in which the Europe of 1992 has been presented as some kind of bean-feast for the central regions of Europe after which the peripheral regions are left with the leftovers'.[15]

The 'Golden Triangle', or the 'Brown Banana'?

As firms and industries rationalise they are more likely to be attracted to areas that are central to the whole of the market and that offer good transport and communications links - for example, to the 'golden triangle', the area bounded by Frankfurt, London and Milan. The UK regions run the risk of ending up not in the 'golden triangle', but in the 'brown banana' of peripheral regions, including Spain, Portugal, Greece and Ireland. The English regions will be further disadvantaged because of the lack of any elected regional structure of government in England that will be able to articulate and lobby for the needs of their areas in the way that regional authorities in other countries are already championing their areas.

The impact of industrial restructuring is likely to be particularly acute in areas of the UK where there is a spatial concentration of vulnerable industries. For example, several local economies are dominated by the motor and aerospace industries and would suffer major dislocation if a plant was relocated, run-down or closed. Other areas of the UK are at a particular disadvantage because of their already very weak economic base. Over 40 per cent of Europe's declining industrial areas are in the UK, as defined by eligibility for the EC Structural Funds under objective two (page 59). A recent survey of Europe's 117 most prosperous cities by Cheshire from the University of Reading found that the UK has only four cities (London, Norwich, Edinburgh and Brighton) in the top 50, while 15 are in the bottom 50 and 8 are in the bottom 20. He concludes that there is now 'very strong statistical evidence that European integration is of much greater benefit to the most central regions of Europe than it is to the more peripheral ones'.[16] Cheshire argues that these results are not inevitable or unchangeable: 'A vigorous urban policy under the aegis of independent regional governments can make a significant impact in improving a city's ranking, wherever it is in the league.'[17]

Summarising the available evidence on the spatial impact of the single European market, commentators have suggested that:

> the completion of the internal market may well exacerbate spatial imbalance in the location of economic activity within the UK and ... this will limit the capacity of the UK to take advantage of the economic changes that are occurring in Europe.[18]

The Changing Labour Market

An important issue in the 1990s will be not just the total number of jobs available and where they are located, but the match between supply and demand for those skills that are likely to be needed in the newly restructured and integrated industries. Rajan[19] has argued that there are six 'time bombs' ticking away in the labour markets of the European states. These are:

- **A numbers gap**, which will arise from the excess of labour demand over labour supply, mainly as a result of the contraction in the size of the 16-24 age group due to demographic changes.

56

- **A skills gap,** which will arise from the new skills required in the new industries at a time when the member states will be suffering from their failure to invest enough in education and training in the crucial decade of the 1980s, when the world economy began to undergo major structural changes.

- **A gender gap,** which arises from the fact that many of the newcomers to the labour market will be mothers returning to work at a time when the new jobs will be in occupations traditionally dominated by men (see Chapter 6).

- **A racial gap,** which arises from the fact that Black and ethnic minority workers will form a growing proportion of the workforce at a time when the new jobs will be in the white-collar occupations, traditionally dominated by White people.

- **A revenue gap,** which arises from the increasing pay-roll costs needed to support the higher proportion of elderly people in the population.

- **A productivity gap,** which arises from the increasing employment in service industries where regular productivity improvements are difficult to generate.

Rajan has also looked at likely future occupational structures in the Europe of the 1990s and has divided jobs into four different groups which are outlined in Box F. The top righthand sector shows occupations where there will be an increasing demand and an increasing need for more skilled workers, while the bottom lefthand sector shows occupations which will be the continuing victims of automation and labour shake-out. The bottom righthand sector shows areas of decline, but where there will need to be an increase in skills. The top lefthand sector shows occupations increasing in numerical size, but contracting in terms of their skills. One result of these changes may be the paradox that some firms in some sectors or some regions may suffer from skill-shortage and difficulties in recruitment, while other employers in other sectors or other regions will be de-skilling their jobs and increasingly relying upon a pool of casual low-paid workers to meet their rising and falling requirements for labour.

Another challenge is that the 16-24 year old age-group, which traditionally has been the main focus of skill training, will contract relatively and absolutely during the 1990s. The largest growth in supply will occur in the older age group, 45-64 year olds, which has suffered skills obsolescence or redundancy or under-employment through previous decades.

QUANTITATIVE AND QUALITATIVE CHANGES IN
OCCUPATIONAL STRUCTURE

	Numbers increasing	
Deskilling	• Secretarial services (P/T) • Junior clericals (P/T) • Recreation services (P/T) • Personal services (P/T) • Supervisors & foremen	• Managers • Engineers, scientists & technologists • IT-related services • Health services • Technicians • Multi-skilled craftsmen • Business specialists • Other professions • Sales & marketing services
	• Junior draftsmen • Single-skilled craftsmen • Operatives • Unskilled occupations • Manual occupations	• Multi-skilled clerks • Supervisors & foremen • Secretarial services • Security services • Recreation services
	Numbers decreasing	**Reskilling**

Source: © Rajan, A., *1992: A Zero Sum Game,* Industrial Society Press, 1990

EC INITIATIVES

The Community has had a long-standing involvement in employment and training initiatives. The SEA and the action programme associated with the Social Charter (page 18) have now provided an additional impetus to EC activity in this field. The main instruments continue to be what are known generically as the EC Structural Funds.[20] These refer to:

• **The European Social Fund (ESF),** which was established in 1958 to promote employment opportunities and geographical and occupational mobility for workers within the Community.

- **The European Regional Development Fund (ERDF)**, which was established in 1975 and mainly gives grants to improve the economic infrastructure of the poorer regions in the Community.

- The guidance section of the **European Agricultural Guidance and Guarantee Fund**, used among other things, to assist a range of rural development schemes throughout the Community.

Until 1989 these three funds operated separately, but the SEA stipulated that they should act to common principles so as to maximise their impact. They now operate as integrated European Structural Funds, with the following five objectives:

1   **Promoting the development and structural adjustment of the less developed regions.** These are regions where GDP per capita is less than 75 per cent of the Community figure averaged over the last three years. This definition covers Greece, much of Spain, Portugal, Southern Italy, Ireland, Northern Ireland and the French Overseas Departments. At least 75 per cent of the European Regional Fund is to go to these areas.

2   **Converting regions and small areas seriously affected by industrial decline.** There are over 30 such regions in the UK, mainly concentrated in Scotland, Wales and the north of England.

3   **Combating long-term unemployment.**

4   **Facilitating the occupational integration of young people.**

5   **Speeding up the adjustment of agricultural structures and promoting the development of rural areas.**[21]

In addition, there is now a more programmatic and integrated approach to the use of the Structural Funds. The emphasis on bringing together different projects within a coherent strategy, and the insistence that a wide range of agencies are involved in an integrated programme of work, is an attempt by the Commission to exercise greater control over the use of funds, and to increase their effectiveness. A further aim is to prevent national governments from using European funds simply to subsidise existing national projects, although doubts have been expressed about the Commission's ability to succeed in this aim. Smaller sums of money have also been set aside for transnational schemes focused on specific themes and issues, and this money will not be subject to the agreement of national governments.

Examples of this more programmatic and thematic approach to the use of the Structural Funds are three programmes developed by the Commission to promote economic regeneration in areas of particular decline: RESIDER (declining steel areas), RENAVAL (declining ship-building areas) and

RECHAR (declining coal-mining areas). The experience of projects funded under the RECHAR programme illustrates one of the main problems of the operation of the Structural Funds in the UK. Even though RECHAR grants are in theory subject to the European Commission's principle of additionality[22], as are all grants from the Structural Funds, UK local authorities have found that in practice they are not being given any national funds to match the European RECHAR funding. The Coalfield Communities Campaign, an alliance of affected local authorities, claims that EC money is 'being used by the British government as an alternative to governmental funding for UK projects'.[23] This has led to threats from the EC to withhold RECHAR funds from the UK. Concern about possible abuse of the additionality principle has also focused on the UK's use of the ESF, where it has been alleged that this was being used as a subsidy to existing employment and training programmes promoted by the then Manpower Services Commission.

The total budget for the Structural Funds has been nearly doubled from 7,400 million ECUs (about £5,180 million) in the 1988 EC budget to 13,000 million ECUs (about £910 million) in 1992 (at 1988 prices). This means that the percentage of the Community budget that is devoted to the Structural Funds will have increased from 18 per cent in 1986 to well over 30 per cent by 1992. However, it is unlikely that much, if any, of this increase will be spent in the UK. The majority of the increase will go to the 'objective one' regions, and the only UK area eligible to benefit from this will be Northern Ireland. For the rest of the UK potential benefits will be concentrated in the 'objective two' regions, and in programmes to assist the long-term unemployed and the young unemployed, as part of an integrated strategy.

The Commission has recently started a number of programmes which use the reformed Structural Funds not to respond to applications from eligible regions or projects within particular member states, but to initiate new cross-national programmes of activity focused on particular themes (Box G). National organisations can only benefit from these programmes if partnerships are formed with at least one other country, and if their proposals are submitted as part of an operational programme co-financed by the member states. The amounts of money allocated are relatively small compared with the major programmes of the Structural Funds. EUROFORM, for example, will get 100 million ECUs (about £70 million) per year for three years; NOW will get 40 million ECUs (about £28 million); and HORIZON 60 million ECUs (about £42 million), compared with the 4.5 billion ECUs (about £3.2 billion) allocated through the ERDF in 1989, and the 3.5 billion ECUs (about £2.5 billion) committed to the ESF in the same years.

As well as programmes that provide direct funding to projects, the Commission supports a number of employment-related information networks and programmes which publicise examples of good practice and

EC INITIATIVES TO FOSTER THE SOCIAL INTEGRATION OF DISADVANTAGED PEOPLE

- NOW is concerned to promote the access of women to employment programmes and to supplement their vocational training. Support can be given to measures that assist the creation of small enterprises and co-operatives by women, and to training and support measures that help women to gain access to employment, including childcare provision.
- HORIZON is aimed at disabled people and other disadvantaged groups and assists in transnational exchanges of good practice.
- EUROFORM. This programme promotes transnational partnerships between people involved in vocational training and assists joint innovative training activity.

More information on these three programmes can be obtained from DG V/C/1 of the European Commission, rue de la Loi 200, B-1049, Brussels.

new ways of working. Again, many of these are relatively small-scale projects in terms of the sums of funding allocated to them. Some of the major programmes are described in Box H. Addresses for further information on these programmes are given in the notes to this chapter.[24]

THE ROLE OF THE VOLUNTARY AND COMMUNITY SECTORS

Making Cross-National Links

Economic developments in the EC provide the context for many of the other policies and areas of concern discussed in this report. In this sense economic and employment changes are important to all voluntary and community organisations, whether or not they are directly involved in action on employment and training issues. The potentially devastating effects of European restructuring on particular industries, geographical regions and local economies will bring a wide range of consequences for the local

MAJOR EC EMPLOYMENT AND TRAINING PROGRAMMES

ERGO The aim of this programme is to stimulate successful experience which can form part of national programmes to combat long-term unemployment. It is designed to complement and reinforce the work of the European Social Fund. Priority is given to the collection of information about local projects and activities, communicated through a regular newsletter, conferences and seminars. There is also a research element to the programme which evaluates projects in the different countries and develops manuals of good practice. The programme comes to an end in 1991 and, at the time of writing, it is not clear if it will continue, and if so, in what form.

LEDA This programme concentrates on building models of local employment development. It has selected 24 areas with very different characteristics - major urban areas, medium-sized towns suffering industrial decline, mixed urban/rural and less developed areas. The areas in the UK are Nottingham and Dundee. LEDA looks at how these areas have developed projects to combat unemployment and then disseminates this information to other local actors and to Community policy makers. It also organises study visits, exchanges and conferences. The programme concentrates on the development of human resources in each area, rather than on the physical environment and infrastructure.

ELISE This is a central source of information on local employment and economic development in the Community. It maintains three databases of information on projects and organisations, and a bibliography of relevant material. It produces a regular magazine and publications on different aspects of employment initiatives.

SYSDEM stands for the European System of Documentation on Employment. Its purpose is to gather available information on employment trends and to provide an interpretation and analysis service to the Commission. SYSDEM also has a central bank of information on employment issues and produces a regular bulletin.

LEADER is a programme for rural development. Its objective is a to create new development structures in rural areas incorporating local community organisations, private interests and statutory agencies. These will be known as 'Rural Development Action Groups' and it is hoped that they will serve as models for all rural areas in the Community. Action groups will draw up business development plans for their areas. Special emphasis is being placed on the use of modern technologies. Measures eligible for funding will include vocational training, employment promotion, rural tourism, assistance for small firms and craft enterprises, and the exploitation and marketing of local products. The budget is 400 million ECUs (about £280 million) and it is expected that contributions will be matched from national and local sources.

SPEC is a support programme for employment creation which was launched in 1990 in response to an initiative from the European Parliament. Its aim is to provide small-scale financial and technical support (5,000-20,000 ECUs, about £3,500-£14,000) to a number of innovatory employment creation projects linked to changes in employment arising from 1992.

Local Employment Initiatives by Women provides one year start-up assistance, and is designed to combat female unemployment and to promote the setting up of businesses by women.

communities concerned. This will change the whole context and climate within which all voluntary and community organisations in those areas have to work. In addition some organisations specifically concerned with employment and training issues will want to respond more directly, not just in terms of economic and employment development, but also in terms of the many different social consequences.

Voluntary and community organisations have many indirect opportunities to influence the general climate of thinking about economic, regional and employment priorities in Europe through their membership of cross-national organisations and pressure groups, and through their consultations with, and lobbying of, MPs, MEPs and the European Commission. However, they can also have a more direct influence upon economic and employment development at a regional and local level. At this level many initiatives are taken by local authorities and other agencies, often in partnership not only with private sector bodies, but also with voluntary and community bodies.

Several local authorities are commissioning studies of the likely impact of European restructuring upon their local economies in order to give early warning of possible changes in jobs, skills and employment and training needs. There is often an opportunity for voluntary and community organisations to contribute to these economic and skills audits by submitting evidence and proposals.

Other local authorities have set up cross-national links with regions and cities in similar circumstances in other parts of Europe, partly to exchange information and establish solidarity, and partly to make sure their interests are adequately represented to the EC and Parliament. These links are sometimes developed in the context of town-twinning programmes, and there may well be opportunities for voluntary and community organisations to take part in these exchanges. Several self-help unemployment fund groups in Wolverhampton, for example, Bushbury Unemployment Group and Bradley Resource Action Group, have been involved in a series of exchange visits with their counterparts at the Dortmund Centre for the Unemployed in Germany, over the past few years. These visits have been supported by grants from Wolverhampton Borough Council, and have proved to be very fruitful in raising consciousness and in developing some joint campaigns.

A third category of responses is coming from groups of local authorities affected by the restructuring of particular industrial sectors. The Coalfields Communities Campaign has already been mentioned. There are also networks for areas concerned with the motor industry (MILAN) and the aerospace industry (AIRLINE).[25] These cross-national initiatives , linking regional and local authorities with a common interest in different parts of the EC, are an innovative response to the sectoral and spatial impacts of the single European market. It will be important for voluntary and community organisations to be aware of these initiatives and to make positive contributions to them wherever possible.

Other voluntary and community organisations will be particularly interested in possible employment and training initiatives and the opportunity to gain funding and cross-national links through one or more of the various European programmes. The challenge for organisations will be to provide unemployed, unskilled and casualised workers with the skills and confidence to allow them to bargain for a better deal in an increasingly polarised labour market. Part of this may involve analysing spheres of employment where skills shortages may arise, and designing high-quality training programmes to match these requirements. Voluntary organisations in Leeds and Sheffield have collaborated with their local authorities in obtaining European funding to set up skill training workshops in computing, electronics, joinery, plastering and other trades, and to provide training to unemployed young people, and women, particularly from Black and ethnic minorities. These have provided flexible childcare, short courses in literacy and numeracy, job placement and counselling, and other forms of practical and social support necessary to make it possible for people who have been out of the labour market to gain the confidence and skills to get good jobs or to go on to further training or higher education.

Working with the European Social Fund

The main source of money for European funding of voluntary-sector job creation and training projects has been the ESF. The UK as a whole provides a large number of training programmes through the ESF and, unlike some member states, has demonstrated an ability to spend its full ESF allocations, although there are unresolved problems over the issue of additionality (page 60). Within the money made available to the UK from the ESF, there are specific allocations for the voluntary sector. In 1991 these are likely to amount to about £20 million, and will account for around 5 per cent of the total funds available to the UK.

The great majority of ESF finance to the voluntary sector in the UK comes through an allocation managed by NCVO. Other allocations are managed by the Women's Training Network and the Industrial Common Ownership Movement. The NCVO allocation is split between programmes for the long-term unemployed, 'objective three' of the Structural Funds, and measures to assist with the integration of young people into the labour market, 'objective four'. Each of these main programmes then has a number of sub-programmes; for example, measures for vocational training, measures for innovatory work for people with disabilities, and measures for the creation of stable jobs by wage subsidies. These overall programmes are agreed with the Commission, and specific applications within each programme are then forwarded by NCVO to the Commission for approval. There has been a great deal of criticism of the time this process has taken, and of the delays in approval and receipt of money that has resulted. However, NCVO have reported that these problems are being overcome, and that in 1992 projects should receive approved grants at the beginning of the year.

NCVO has serviced the ESF Information Network (ESFIN) providing regular mailings and briefings, as well as conferences and co-ordination of voluntary sector lobbying on ESF matters. This network is now being combined with other NCVO networks on employment into a Training and Employment Network for Voluntary Organisations. This network is likely to have up to 1,000 contacts.

NCVO runs its ESF programme in conjunction with a UK ESF Steering Committee. The Committee is made up of regional representatives elected at regional meetings of all groups receiving ESF funding.

There are two important developments in European thinking about the use of the Structural Funds which will have increasing implications for the voluntary and community sectors. The first is the trend within much Community thinking towards 'regionalisation'. This is reflected in the Structural Funds by increasing priority being given to disadvantaged regions, particularly the under-developed and poorer regions in the south of the Community. Within the UK the private sector and local authorities tend to support these developments. Voluntary organisations have reacted to these developments and, as a result, the NCVO voluntary sector programme is to be run on a regional basis in the future. Regional networks and offices will be established, and the servicing of the regional programmes will also be carried out on a regional basis, rather than by NCVO nationally. There is some concern among voluntary organisations that if larger-scale regional projects are favoured, then the needs of special groups such as the long-term unemployed will be marginalised.

The second development is more recent, and may appear to contradict the first. Some evidence is beginning to emerge, notably in a key policy document *Europe 2000: Outlook for the Development of the Community's Territory*[26] that in the next review of the Structural Funds the Commission may want to shift some of its funding away from regions defined as eligible through specific criteria of need, for example, levels of investment and unemployment, and towards themes, issues and programmes defined on a cross-national basis, and initiated by the Commission. This trend is already apparent in the rapid growth in the number of cross-national programmes and initiatives promoted by the EC, for example RECHAR, RENAVEL, and EUROFORM. If these policy trends develop further, then voluntary organisations will have to learn even more how to build working links with their counterparts in other countries, and to engage with the Commission's priority themes if they are to receive funding.

CONCLUSION

This chapter has highlighted some of the main economic and employment changes which may take place in Europe and the UK over the next decade, as part of the moves towards a more integrated and competitive European market. It has identified some of the industrial sectors, regions, and localities which the EC and other commentators consider to be most at risk. It has discussed possible changes in the labour market, in terms of numbers and types of jobs and skills, and has considered their impact on vulnerable groups and areas.

The chapter also described the European Structural Funds, ESF, the ERDF, and the Agricultural Fund, which are being used to cushion some of the consequences of these economic and employment changes, and to try to integrate disadvantaged areas and groups more fully into the mainstream labour market. Some of the newer European employment and training schemes and initiatives have also been reviewed, and the practical challenges and opportunities facing the voluntary and community sectors in relation to employment and training issues in the Europe of the 1990s have been identified.

REFERENCES

1   Commission of the European Communities (1990) *Employment in Europe*. Directorate General Employment Industrial Relations and Social Affairs. COM(90) 290 final.

2   Cecchini, *The European Challenge*.

3   Neuberger, H. (1989) 'The Economics of 1992' *Local Government Policy Making*, December 16:3 pp3-10.

4   Cecchini, *The European Challenge*.

5   Buignes, P., Ilzkovitz, F., Lebran, S. (1990) *The Impact of the Internal Market by Industrial Sector: the Challenge for the Member States*. Social Europe special issue. Luxembourg.

6   EC press release.

7   Grahl and Teague, *1992 The Big Market*.

8   Rajan, A. (1990) *1992 A Zero Sum Game: Business, Know-How, and Training Challenges in an Integrated Europe*. Industrial Society Press.

9   Quoted in *The Financial Times*, 1 December, 1988.

10   The Financial Times, 21 October, 1988.

11   Emerson, M. et al (1988) *The Economics of 1992: The EC Commission's Assessment of the Economic Effects of Completing the Internal Market*, OUP.

12   Rajan, *1992 A Zero Sum Game*.

13   Neuberger, 'The Economics of 1992'.

14   Cameron, G. et al (eds) (1991) 'The economic outlook for the regions and countries of the United Kingdom in the 1990s', *Cambridge Economic Review*.

15   EC press release of Bruce Millan's speech to the London Executive Committee of the Scottish Council for Development and Industry on 19 March, 1990.

16   Cheshire, P. (1990) 'Explaining the recent performance of the European Community's major urban regions'. *Urban Studies* 27 pp311-333.

17   Cheshire, 'Explaining the recent performance of the European Community's major urban regions'.

18   Cameron, *The Economic Outlook*.

19   Rajan, 1992: *A Zero-Sum Game*.

20   The description given is very brief and does not cover the complexities of the Structural Funds and their re-organisation. A more detailed description can be found in Davison and Seary, *Grants from Europe*; CEC (1989) *Guide to the Reform of the Community's Structural Funds* (CB-56-89-223-EN-C); CEC (1990) *The new structural policies of the European Community*, European File 7 August 1990.

21   This description of the objectives of the Structural Funds is taken from Davison and Seary, *Grants from Europe*.

22   The principle of 'additionality' is that EC funds must be genuinely additional to existing national and local budgets, and not used as a substitute or subsidy for them.

23   *The Guardian*, 22 February 1991.

24   ERGO *Work Again and other documents, including regular newsletter*, produced by CEI Consultants Ltd and PA Cambridge Economic Consultants on behalf of the European Commission. Available from DGV/B/1 of the Commission, or CEI Consultants Ltd, rue Belliard 205, B-1040, Brussels, or PA Cambridge Consultants, 62 Hills Rd, Cambridge, CB2 1LA.
      LEDA *Reports and regular newsletters*, produced by Local and Regional Development Planning for the European Commission (DGV) Available from LRDP, rue Franklin, 106, B-1040, Brussels.
      ELISE *Papers and newsletters*, produced by the European Association for Information on Local Development for the European Commission (DGV) Available from ELISE, rue Breydel 34, B-1040, Brussels.
      SYSDEM *Bulletins*, produced by ECOTEC Research and Consulting Limited for the European Commission (DGV) Available from ECOTEC, 28-34 Albert Street, Birmingham B4 7UD.
      SPEC details from DGV/B/1 of the Commission, or the International Union of Local Authorities (IULA) PO Box 90646, 2509 LP The Hague, Netherlands.
      Details on Employment Initiatives by women can be obtained from DGV/B/4 Equal Opportunities Unit of the Commission, or Maire O'Leary, PO Box 1, Galway, Ireland.

25   Further information about these two networks can be obtained from The Local Government Centre, Warwick University, Coventry CV4 7AL.

26   CEC (1991) *Europe 2000: Outlook for the Development of the Community's Territory*. A preliminary overview. Communication from the

Commission to the Council and the European Parliament.
CX-60-90-377-EN-C Brussels.

4

Social Welfare, Poverty and Disadvantage

INTRODUCTION

This chapter looks at the effect of European integration on social needs, on the welfare systems of member states, including their social protection and social assistance policies[1], and on poverty and the disadvantaged. Will there be any changes in the population groups most in need or at risk as a result of 1992? Will poverty decline or increase? Is 1992 going to mean the emergence of a pan-European welfare state? Will social protection and social assistance systems be harmonised throughout the member states? What are the implications for voluntary and community organisations concerned with such issues?

One of the contradictions in the whole debate about the prospects for a 'social Europe' is the way in which it is possible to find equally strong evidence either to support Jacques Delors' prediction that by the year 2000 the EC will be responsible for some 80 per cent of economic and social legislation,[2] or to conclude that very little has or will be achieved by the EC in the social welfare field.

So, what really is the scope for EC action in social policy? The EC currently has very limited legal powers in terms of social welfare policy (page 16) and although there is much discussion about the possible expansion of EC competence into the social field through revision of the treaties (Box B, Chapter 1), it seems likely that legal responsibility for social welfare will remain primarily within the national domain for the foreseeable future. Factors which would make legislative change extremely difficult include: the conflicting political interests at member state level, the extreme practical, political, and social complexity of bringing together welfare systems that are deeply rooted in the different cultures of member states (Box I), and the vast financial costs that would be involved.

In spite of the limitation in its powers of competence, the Commission is increasingly taking specific social policy initiatives, either to cushion the negative consequences of the more competitive market, or in response to lobbying from the social partners and pressure groups. In addition, lively and important debates are occurring within the EC about whether the moves towards a more integrated European economy should be accompanied by equally strong moves towards a more integrated welfare system, what such a system should and would look like, and what the implications of a more integrated approach to social policy would be for various aspects of need.[3]

The Debates about European Social Policy

It is possible to identify three dimensions to the current debates. Firstly, there is the crucial question of the relative roles of the EC and of national and local governments in social policy. How far should the EC get involved in social welfare policies that have traditionally been the responsibility of national and local governments? On what basis should decisions be made about the division of responsibilities between the different levels of government - European, national and local? This dimension of the debate is underpinned by broad political and ideological views about the future of Europe, issues of subsidiarity and of national sovereignty (see Chapters 1 and 10).

Secondly, there is the question of whether rights to social protection and assistance, and to social welfare generally, should be attached to an individual's employment status or to citizenship. In the majority of member states, eligibility for social protection and assistance is more heavily dependent upon employment insurances or other job-related qualifications than in the UK, where traditionally the welfare state has also emphasised the right to assistance based upon social need. (In practice this is less and less the case in the UK, as right to social security benefits is increasingly linked to conditions about re-insertion into the labour market through involvement in temporary employment schemes.) Some commentators fear that the SEA will further increase the likelihood of employment becoming the main basis of eligibility for welfare entitlements rather than citizenship status or even residence. They question the moral as well as the financial viability of the employment-centred model of the welfare state, arguing instead for a welfare state with rights and obligations based upon citizenship, and one which guarantees its citizens an unconditional, tax-financed basic income.[4] Townsend, for example, has argued that the implementation of the Social Charter will result in a widening of the difference between the status of workers and those who are not in work:

71

The [EC] policy emerging is workerist and corporatist.... [and] has implications over the life span. It favours the middle-aged and the prosperous, especially those well entrenched within employing organisations. This will tend to exacerbate the inequalities in living standards between the middle-aged and the elderly on the one hand, and the young and young adults rearing children on the other.[5]

Thirdly, there is the question of whether greater integration of European welfare systems would mean a levelling up or levelling down of social benefits across the Community.[6] Compared with the UK, the safety nets of income and social support for those who fall outside the mainstream labour market are set low and narrow in many member states, and assistance for those in need is often provided mainly through philanthropic or religious organisations rather than by the state (Box I). There is a general concern that the minimum standards in Europe could all too easily become the overall standards. These are not abstract questions. They have very practical implications for the growing number of people in poverty in Europe.

A New Poverty in Europe?

The poverty confronting the European member states in the 1990s differs from earlier patterns of poverty both in terms of scale and composition. It now affects very much larger numbers of people within the population. A study for the European Commission in 1988 estimated that the numbers of people in poverty in Europe (defined as less than 50 per cent of average equivalent income for each country) had risen from 38.6 million in the period 1973-1977 (12.8 per cent of the population) to 43.9 million (13.9 per cent of the population) in 1984-1985.[7] A later report by Eurostat, using the above definition of poverty, came up with even higher estimates: 49.7 million people in poverty in the 12 member states in 1985.[8] The Eurostat figures for the UK are particularly striking. The numbers of people in poverty in the UK have risen from 8.2 million (14.6 per cent of the population) in 1980 to 10.3 million (18.2 per cent of the population) in 1985. This gives the UK the largest number of people in poverty in all the EC member states, and the fifth highest percentage, putting it in the same league as Greece, Spain and Ireland. The UK also had by far the largest number of households in poverty (3.8 million) in Europe in 1985, and apart from Portugal, the highest percentage (18.9 per cent). In 1985 the UK therefore accounted for almost one-fifth of all the people and households in the EC living below their respective national poverty lines.

The profile of poverty in Europe differs from previous patterns of poverty in its scope as well as its scale. In many European countries, poverty now affects much wider sections of the population than before. It includes people from a wider range of age, gender, race, class, and skill categories. For example

BOX I

MODELS OF WELFARE WITHIN EUROPE

Abrahamson has identified four different models and traditions of welfare operating within the European countries (not just the EC member states):

- The **rudimentary** welfare state (or Catholic social policy), associated with Spain, Portugal and Italy. This model emphasises philanthropic solutions to welfare provision by traditional institutions such as the church, family and private charity, with limited public welfare institutions and policies developing alongside, to fill in any gaps in provision.

- The **institutional** welfare state (or corporatist social policy), associated with Germany and central European countries. This model emphasises labour market solutions where employers and employees have agreed upon arrangements covering workers in the case of unemployment, sickness and old age. The parts of the population left outside the labour market are much less well protected and may be dependent upon local public or private charity.

- The **residual** welfare state (or liberal social policy), associated with the UK. The boundaries of the welfare state are rolled back, and public services are contracted out to the private and voluntary sectors. People are encouraged to look primarily to the private market or the family to meet their needs. The state is reduced to being a final safety net, rather than a primary provider.

- The **modern** welfare state (or social democratic policy), associated with the Scandinavian countries. This model is characterised by a high degree of universal services with emphasis on the public sector as main provider, although increasingly the emphasis is on voluntary or commercial organisations joining the welfare mix.

Source: Abrahamson, P. (1991) *Social Policy in Europe Towards Year 2000: Social Integration or Social Differentiation*, Roskilde University, PO Box 260 DK-4000 Roskilde

in the early 1970s pensioners accounted for the highest percentage of those in poverty, but they have now been overtaken by people of working age. Although elderly people still form one of the most significant groups in poverty, the unemployed and particularly the long-term unemployed now form a far greater proportion (Box J).

THE CHANGING PROPORTIONS OF ELDERLY AND UNEMPLOYED PEOPLE WITHIN THE POPULATION OF THOSE IN POVERTY

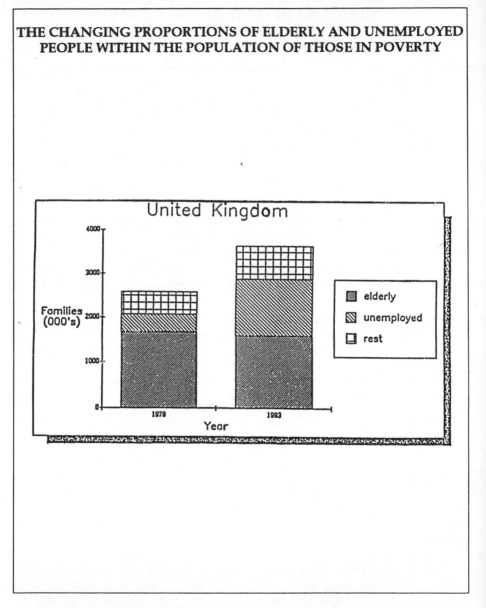

Source: Room, G. et al (1987) *Action to Combat Poverty: The Experience of 65 Projects*, CASP, University of Bath

Changes in social and family structures have also had an impact on the composition of those in poverty, and single-parent households now feature more significantly among those suffering from economic and social marginalisation.[9] The net effect of these two trends (greater numbers of unemployed people and single-parent households in poverty) has been to bring an increasing number of children and young people into poverty.[10] The UK experienced a 12 per cent increase in the number of poor children between 1980 and 1985.[11]

These differences in the composition of those in poverty have led some commentators, including the Commission, to coin the term 'new poverty' to describe the poverty facing Europe in the 1990s. Some voluntary organisations are concerned that the invention and use of this term may serve to mask the persistent problems of traditional groups in poverty, such as elderly and homeless people, and may reopen distinctions between the deserving and undeserving poor. However, the term 'new poverty' is useful if it highlights the way in which poverty can no longer be treated as a marginal welfare issue, as it often was in the 1960s and 1970s, but must be seen as a mainstream issue for both economic and social policy in Europe.

The Ageing of the European Population

Another major challenge for European social policy is the dramatic ageing of the population. The number of those aged over 65 in Europe has been increasing rapidly from 34 million in 1950 (8.7 per cent of the population), to 61 million in 1985 (12.4 per cent of the population), and is predicted to reach 97 million by 2025 (18.4 per cent of the population).[12]

The ageing of the European population is partly the result of an increase in average life expectancy, and partly the result of a fall in the birth rate. Table 4 shows the effect of such trends for Britain: if the birth rate remains low then the worker-pensioner ratio in Britain would fall by about 35 per cent between 2000 and 2030. And, compared with other European member states, the UK already has one of the heaviest dependency ratios (the population over 60 and under 15 as a percentage of the population aged between 15 and 59 (Table 5).

A rapidly ageing population structure, combined with a decrease in the proportion of wage-earners to dependants, poses great challenges for economic and social policy. One of the central questions is how to provide and/or pay for the pensions, social assistance, and specialised services (housing, transport, leisure, social work, health care and hospital or domiciliary services) needed by an elderly clientele, compared with the very different pattern of welfare services which has been required by the predominantly young and family-centred population structure of the post-war period.

TABLE 4

NUMBERS OF WORKERS PER PENSIONER

Number of workers per pensioner

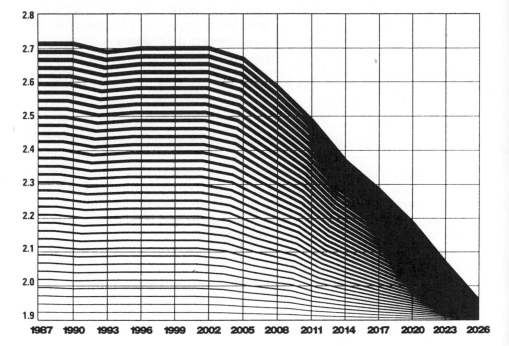

Source: Ermisch, J. (1990) *Fewer Babies: Longer Lives*, p44. Joseph Rowntree Foundation, York

76

TABLE 5

DEPENDENCY RATIOS BY COUNTRIES: 1970 - 2000 ACCORDING TO THE 'MOST LIKELY' VARIANT (POPULATION AGED LESS THAN 15 AND 60 AND OVER PER 100 POPULATION AGED 15-59)

Country	1970	1975	1980	1985	1990	1995	2000
Denmark	69	70	69	67	67	66	65
Finland	63	60	55	54	54	53	51
Ireland	88	87	88	88	86	82	76
Norway	74	75	75	74	72	69	65
Sweden	68	72	73	74	72	69	68
United Kingdom	75	76	74	73	73	70	68
Austria	81	78	66	63	63	62	62
Belgium	74	72	64	64	66	67	66
France	75	75	68	69	70	69	67
Germany, Federal Republic	74	72	61	57	59	61	65
Netherlands	72	69	66	65	66	63	61
Switzerland	72	70	67	67	68	67	65

Source: United Nations: Post-war demographic trends in Europe and the outlook until the year 2000. Economic Survey of Europe in 1974, Table VII.17, Part II of the Economic Commission for Europe (ECE), Geneva. New York 1975.

THE EFFECTS OF THE SINGLE EUROPEAN MARKET

What will be the effects of the single European market upon social need and poverty in Europe, and on the groups most vulnerable to poverty? It is of course difficult to distinguish the specific effects of the single European market from more general economic and social trends. It is even more difficult to forecast future trends. Furthermore, we do not yet know the extent to which EC initiatives in the social field will, or will not, be successful in countering the harsher effects of a more competitive European market.

We can, however, forecast continuing changes in the age structure of the population. The increase in the number of pensioners-per-worker could lead to a further fiscal crisis in Europe, as member states struggle to support increased claims on social assistance and other forms of public expenditure from a reduced tax base.

The more pessimistic scenarios for 1992 outlined in Chapter 3 suggest that the single European market could also lead to substantial increases in unemployment in particular regions of the EC, specifically those regions peripheral to the 'golden triangle' (page 13). These twin processes (increases in need as a result of demographic trends plus potential increases in unemployment) have led some commentators to argue that 1992 could result in further increases in poverty in Europe during the 1990s, with major implications for those organisations working to combat poverty.[13]

The extent and nature of migration which will occur post-1992 is less clear, as are the effects that migration will have on the geographical distribution of social need and poverty. One possibility is that the more skilled and qualified workers will move towards the 'golden triangle', and that the better-off and more-active elderly will head towards sunnier climates in southern European countries. The result could be that an even more disadvantaged and dependent population is left behind in the peripheral regions of the UK, creating greater demands on already over-stretched welfare services in these regions. And, if workers take up the opportunities offered by the free movement of labour in 1992 to move about Europe in search of new jobs, what new housing needs, to take just one example of changing welfare needs, will this bring? The European Federation of National Organisations Working with the Homeless (FEANTSA) has predicted that:

> we now face... a great migration into the centre of Europe, a massive depopulation of the peripheral economies... That kind of upheaval has produced homelessness in the past, it's already doing so, and this

argument leaves aside the appalling level of homelessness we already face in Europe before we all arrive at the promised land of 1992.[14]

A further unknown dimension of social need and poverty is the extent of immigration of non-Europeans, and what effects such immigration would have on economic and social policy in Europe.   Robbins and Room have raised the question of whether 'immigration from Eastern Europe, or from North Africa (will) replace the demographic shortfall which might otherwise improve opportunities for currently disadvantaged groups?' They conclude: 'in short, we do not know whether a Europe without boundaries will be the exciting, prosperous place that is sometimes presented in Commission literature, or a place of increasing uncertainty and polarisation'.[15]

In purely economic terms, the integrated European market of 325 million people will certainly be undermined if nearly 50 million (15 per cent) of them are too poor to consume the goods and services offered in that market. Equally, the cost of public expenditure to support a large number of unemployed, elderly, migrant and poor people would be a heavy burden on the newly emerging European state, whose working-age labour force of 133 million is already less than half the total population. Fundamental issues such as these pose major economic, social and moral questions for the emerging European market and Community, and are at the heart of the battle of competing ideas, interests and values within the emerging European welfare state.

EC INITIATIVES

Social Protection and Assistance

The Social Charter (page 18) is seen by some as providing a cautious but important step towards greater Community involvement in member states' systems of social protection and assistance, by stating 'the right of each worker to adequate social protection and an adequate level of social security benefits'. Furthermore, it states that 'persons who have been unable either to enter or re-enter the labour market and have no means of subsistence must be able to receive sufficient resources and social assistance in keeping with their particular situation'.

In May 1991, as part of its action programme to implement the Social Charter, the Commission adopted a recommendation on 'common criteria concerning sufficient resources and social assistance in the social protection systems' of member states.[16]   The recommendation indicates the Commission's determination to establish a common safety net of tax-based social assistance in all member states (Portugal, Spain, Italy and Greece currently have no such scheme) to complement insurance-based systems of social protection. It will be submitted for adoption by the Council of Ministers by the end of 1991. If adopted, it would not represent any significant advance in policy or provision in the UK (where a safety net of social assistance for those not covered by national insurance benefits already exists, albeit in residual form). However, it implies an active role for the European Commission in promoting the generalisation of such rights across the member states, and in incorporating them into a more coherent European policy for combating social exclusion. The proposals fall far short of the concept of basic income which some pressure groups are campaigning for, but go some way towards establishing the EC's role in recommending that member states guarantee a minimum income. (By basic income is understood a general obligation on behalf of society to provide every citizen with the necessary means of subsistence, irrespective of whether they work or not, whereas a guaranteed minimum income refers to a differential, means-tested allowance linked to labour market reinsertion.)[17]

Other tangible achievements of the EC in the field of social protection have been the co-ordination of benefits at a rather technical level for migrant workers,[18] and the directives aimed at the equal treatment of men and women in social security schemes (page 107).

The European Programmes to Combat Poverty

A key strand of EC involvement in the area of poverty and disadvantage, aside from the Structural Funds described in Chapter 3, has been the funding, over a period of more than 15 years, of three successive anti-poverty programmes.

The first two anti-poverty programmes (1975-1980 and 1985-1989) consisted of a number of small-scale projects, largely sponsored by voluntary and community organisations. For example, the second European programme funded 91 action-research projects concerned with long-term unemployment, young unemployed, elderly people, single parent families, migrants and refugees, marginals, integrated action in rural areas, and integrated action in urban areas.[19]

A key conclusion from the experience and evaluation of the first and second anti-poverty programmes was that small-scale local voluntary and community projects needed to be linked in much more closely to the local and national government bodies which control the main resources, policies and institutions that shape the lives of the poor.

The third European programme to combat poverty, which began in late 1989, was designed to build upon the lessons learned in previous projects. It is a five-year programme involving 27 'model action' projects and 12 'innovatory projects', supported by a network of national research and development units (RDUs) and a central European team of specialist advisers. The aim is to move from small-scale grassroots projects towards larger 'prototype' projects operating at the level of mainstream agencies. The challenge is to co-ordinate the policies and practices of agencies that have the power and resources to tackle some of the local causes of poverty, and to harness these to the initiatives and priorities of local community organisations.

The third European programme has defined six key concepts which are significant not only in what they reveal about the EC's aims in tackling poverty, but also in identifying the more general assumptions behind the Commission's emerging social policies. They are therefore discussed in some depth.

Partnership

The first and principal concept is partnership. Public, private, voluntary and community-based agencies are asked to set up an interagency steering committee to oversee the development and implementation of each local project in the programme. The partners are also responsible for raising funds to match the EC's 50 per cent grant. The concept of partnership means more than organisations simply coming together to sponsor an application to the EC, or to act as an arm's-length management committee presiding over the distribution of grants for community projects. Partners are intended to be the main actors in developing and implementing an interagency strategy to combat poverty. In the Pilton (Edinburgh) Project, for example, the partnership committee consists of Lothian Regional Council, Edinburgh District Council, the Scottish Office, the Scottish Development Agency (the main economic development agency in Scotland), and a private sector company called World Markets, which has its headquarters on the edge of the project area.

Participation

The second key concept is that of participation by representatives of the target groups in the project areas, in the planning, development, management and implementation of the strategy to combat poverty. The linking of the top-down strategic planning processes of agencies controlling the resources and services to the bottom-up initiatives of local community organisations is neither easy nor uncontroversial. The Liverpool Granby Project, for example, has to address the deep scepticism of local community organisations (many of them Black) who have been on the receiving-end of 20 years of research studies and special pilot programmes, but who feel that they and their area have received little practical benefit in terms of improved conditions. The Confederation of Black Organisations and other local groups now have a majority of the places on the management committee of the project and play an active role in trying to influence the strategy and priorities for the project.

Interagency strategy
Interagency strategy is the third key concept. The programme's intention is to promote strategies which add up to more than the collection of innovative projects which characterised the previous anti-poverty programmes. Partner organisations are involved in analysing the distinctive nature and dynamics of poverty in their specific project area. They are expected to map and review all the actions undertaken by their own and other agencies which have an impact (positive or negative) on poverty and deprivation in the project area. They are required to develop a strategy linking the relevant public, private and voluntary agencies in a co-ordinated programme of action which takes account of the specific features of poverty in the project area, eliminates any overlap or contradictions in policy between the various agencies, and develops new interagency initiatives to tackle unmet needs.

Multi-dimensional poverty
The fourth key concept is that of multi-dimensional poverty. This is based on the finding from previous action-research that those in poverty are often trapped in a vicious circle of deprivation in which loss of one resource or service can lead to the loss of several others. For example, people losing their jobs not only suffer a sudden loss of income and social status, but may also experience mortgage or rent arrears, leading to loss of housing, ill-health, family or marital breakdown, and erosion of social support networks. Equally, geographical areas in which there is loss of private or public investment can suffer social decline, with poorer quality housing, education, transport and leisure services, communal facilities for childcare, and poorer shopping facilities.

Economic and social integration
The fifth concept is that of economic and social integration. A lesson of the earlier programmes is that there is no point in developing programmes of social support and skill-training for the unemployed if there are no jobs for them to go to. Economic and social integration means that skill-training programmes must be devised to fit both the needs and potential of the unemployed *and* the skill shortages and employment needs of local employers (private and public).

Additionality
Finally, the sixth key concept utilised by Poverty 3 is additionality, described earlier in Chapter 3 (page 60).

Although the European anti-poverty programmes do not amount to a European social policy for disadvantaged groups, they have provided funding for a wide range of local authorities, voluntary and community organisations and other bodies involved in social action projects, and have offered important models for other similar work in the UK. However, as Townsend points out,[20] it is necessary to see the initiatives in perspective. The budget for the third European programme is 55 million ECUs (approximately £38.5 million) spread over a period of five years –less than the *annual* budget of many social services departments in the UK. The enormous scale of poverty in Europe has meant that the European Parliament and the Economic and Social Committee (Appendix C) have expressed considerable impatience with what they see as a lack of progress by the Commission in the anti-poverty field.[21] The Commission's response has been to point out that it is the member states, through the Council of Ministers, that have constantly restricted the budget and the scope of the anti-poverty programmes. The UK at one stage even challenged the use of the word 'poverty' in the title of the third European programme, and it is rumoured that civil servants in the Department of Social Security have been reduced to referring to 'the P word'!

Research on Poverty and Disadvantage

One consequence of the EC's limited competence to initiate action in the social welfare field has been its involvement in the sponsoring and publishing of various research initiatives. The programmes to combat poverty have been accompanied by related research and statistical studies which have produced a wealth of documentation.[22] For the third programme, 6-9 per cent of the budget is devoted to such work.

At the beginning of 1990, the Commission established an observatory (page 21) on policies to combat social exclusion, gradually coming to be called the Poverty Observatory. This runs in parallel with the Poverty 3 programme, although it is not funded by it.[23] The observatory has conducted a feasibility study concerned with the nature of and processes creating marginalisation and social exclusion in all member states.[24]

Another relevant EC sponsored agency is the European Foundation for the Improvement of Living and Working Conditions. Although much of its work is employment related, some of its programmes are relevant to social policy and disadvantage. For example, it has conducted a multi-national study on 'Coping with Social and Economic Change at Neighbourhood Level'.[25] This investigated the role and contribution of local community action in responding to social and economic problems. The focus was on disadvantaged urban areas and the links between the actions of households, groups and organisations, and policymakers in the public, private and voluntary sectors. The research was developed through institutes in Ireland, Belgium, Netherlands and the UK, where the Community Development Foundation played a major role.

Initiatives Concerning Elderly People

Since the social provisions of the Treaty of Rome concentrate on measures for workers, there is no obvious legal base to justify direct action for elderly people. The main focus to date has been on retirement issues, which can be justified in terms of their relation to work. A non-binding recommendation on flexible retirement policies in member states was adopted in 1982. This provided for more age flexibility, the right of older workers to compensation for reduced working hours, the right to have paid employment in retirement, and pre-retirement preparation programmes.

In recent years, however, the growing debate on the ageing of Europe's population has meant that the EC is recognising the need for wider action in relation to elderly people. In addition, Eurolink Age (see next section) has put persistent pressure on the European institutions for more initiatives in favour of elderly people. In 1991 the EC established a cross-national observatory on elderly people,[26] drawing together researchers in each of the member states to monitor demographic trends and developments in policy relating to elderly people. It will look at the interaction between ageing and social and economic policy and will examine dimensions such as income and quality of life, older people and the labour market, health and social services, and social integration.

The result of this increasing attention on elderly people has been that in November 1990 the first programme of Community action for elderly people was agreed (to run 1991-1993, Box K). Although this has been termed an 'action' programme, activities are in fact limited to research, information gathering and exchange, again highlighting the difficulties of extending the powers of the EC in the social field.[27]

Finally, the Social Charter devotes a section to elderly people, stating that 'elderly persons who are not entitled to a pension and who have no other adequate resources should receive a minimum income and social and medical assistance adapted to their needs'. This has less immediate relevance to elderly people in the UK, where minimum pension rights are currently ensured by the State, but it has considerable significance in other European countries without these safety nets.

BOX K

ACTIONS FOR ELDERLY PEOPLE TO BE CARRIED OUT BY THE COMMUNITY 1991-93

European Year of the Elderly and Solidarity between generations

The Commission proposes that 1993 be designated as the European Year of the Elderly.

Studies and knowledge transfer

- internal market (socio-medical services, housing and living conditions);
- regional development, consumer affairs, tourism;
- income (especially elderly women and migrants);
- handicap in old age;
- contribution of elderly people to the economic and social environment (especially re: education and training and the development of social and cultural services.

Organisation of events and exchange of information (meetings/conferences/seminars)

- elderly people's positive contribution to economic, social and cultural life (social and voluntary work);
- effects of the ageing of the active population in the labour market;
- the costs of elderly people on social security budgets.

Preparation for networking of innovative experiences

- exploration of the feasibility of setting up a European network of action projects;
- creation of an EC Consultative Committee composed of two representatives from each Member State, plus a Liaison Group composed of European organisations concerned with elderly people.

Source: *Eurolink Age Bulletin,* July 1990

Initiatives Concerning Disabled People

The World Health Organisation (WHO) estimates that 10 per cent of the population of the European Community is disabled (about 34 million people). Actions to assist disabled people have been easier for the Commission to justify within the restrictions of legal competence, because of the possibility of linking initiatives to the needs of disabled *workers* (even though much of the work supported is in fact for disabled people *outside* the workforce). Some initiatives for disabled people are supported by the ESF (page 58), and there are also some projects about the use of new technology to assist disabled people in various EC research and development programmes.

The main focus of EC involvement in this area has been the funding of two action programmes, with a third expected to run from 1992-1996. In 1988 the Council adopted the second programme, known as HELIOS (Handicapped People in the European Community Living Independently in an Open Society).[28] Included in the HELIOS programme are the activities under the programme of European collaboration on the integration of disabled children into ordinary schools, which the Council agreed in 1987. Also included are four networks: a network of rehabilitation centres and three networks of 'local model activities', concerned with employment, independent living and education. In addition, there is an information technology initiative called HANDYNET - a multi-lingual information system on disability questions dealing with technical aids. The Commission has also been promoting policy instruments covering employment and various aspects of independent living, such as transport, access to buildings and housing.[29] Finally, the EC has allocated 180 million ECUs (about £126 million) from the Structural Funds to the HORIZON programme, which aims to improve the integration of the handicapped and disadvantaged into the labour market (Box G, Chapter 3).

Initiatives Concerning Housing and Homelessness

The restructuring of capital and labour markets, the exposure of public contracts to more open competitive tendering, and many other aspects of the 1992 programme all have potential impact on the patterns of housing need and the processes of housing production and distribution.

The Commission undertakes little action in the area of housing, and explains this in terms of its limited competence (but see page 16). The Local Government Information Bureau believe that: 'this could change, however, if the Social Charter programme were to be extended to include subsidised housing; the Commission and European Parliament would thus have more possibilities of tabling proposals in this area, such as initiating a specific programme for public housing under the European Social Fund'.[30] There is already a European liaison committee for social housing (CECODHAS), which represents the interests of housing associations, and acts as a vehicle for an exchange of experience between different countries.

Other commentators, however, believe that the Commission will not get involved in the social policy aspects of housing at all, but will limit its role to the economic aspects, by opening up the contracts for the construction of housing projects to competitive tender across the member states.

To date, the only direct EC action in this field has been the provision of loans at low rates of interest for the construction, purchase and modernisation of housing for workers in the coal and steel industries;[31] the inclusion of some homelessness projects within the 'marginals' theme of the second European anti-poverty programme;[32] some financial support to FEANTSA (European Federation of National Organisations Working with the Homeless, see next section); some studies and reports on homelessness in Europe;[33] and some meetings of EC housing ministers, where no commitments appear to have been made.

THE ROLE OF THE VOLUNTARY AND COMMUNITY SECTORS

The past few years have seen a dramatic growth in voluntary sector activity at a European level, particularly in the anti-poverty field. Many organisations are becoming increasingly aware that although the EC is still predominantly an economic community, it has opened up a number of social welfare issues to debate and action.

In December 1990 a European anti-poverty network (EAPN)[34] was launched in Brussels. Forty delegates from the UK attended the inaugural conference, elected by voluntary and community organisations on a regional basis. The aim of the network is to bring together voluntary and community groups committed to combating poverty to organise and mobilise across Europe.

The evolution of this network highlights some important issues for voluntary and community organisations. Although drawing upon the momentum developed by previous national networks (in this country, for example, the UK Poverty Forum), the EAPN was initiated and financed by the European Commission, as part of their growing recognition of the importance of drawing voluntary organisations into the EC policy-making process. This means that, from the start, the EAPN has a legitimacy at a European level, and structures for dialogue between the Commission and voluntary organisations are well established. But it also means that the development of the network has been essentially a 'top-down' rather than 'bottom-up' process, and this has led to a concern among some organisations that the network does not reflect grassroots' initiatives and priorities.

There are two important implications for UK voluntary and community organisations of EC involvement in anti-poverty work. Firstly, the EC has been a significant source of funding for some projects, and has thus enabled more grassroots anti-poverty work to take place in the UK at a time when the national government has shown hostility to such work, and indeed, has denied that there is any real poverty remaining in the UK.[35] Of course, working within an environment where national government policies may run counter to the aims of projects funded by European institutions (of which the national government are a part), carries with it its own set of difficulties.[36]

Secondly, the EC has provided alternative models for anti-poverty work, and an alternative ideological framework within which voluntary organisations can work. The European anti-poverty programmes have been influenced more by French than UK welfare ideology, and are characterised by attempts to prevent poverty through the maintenance of living standards and, more generally, the integration of the poor into mainstream society through solidarity measures such as universal benefits, and through skill-training. This is in stark contrast to present welfare philosophy in the UK, where there is an increasing emphasis on individuals meeting their own needs through self-help and the market, with the back up of a means-tested safety net.[37]

There are many other examples of voluntary organisation activity in European social welfare issues. Eurolink Age has been involved for many years in European lobbying and providing an information service concerning elderly people in the EC. It has a Brussels-based office, and uses the services of a European consultant to develop its lobbying policy and practice. This has enabled it to help establish a European parliamentary intergroup (Appendix C) on ageing, which has proved a key source of support in lobbying for more Community funds for elderly people. Eurolink Age's priorities in the next two years are to promote the concept of elderly people as a positive resource, and to promote action projects, and intergenerational work. They have also been active in work on elderly people and disability.[38]

The Single Parent Action Network (SPAN) is an attempt to build a cross-national network of self-help groups concerned with the needs of single parents. It grew out of, and builds on, the work of the Bristol One Parent Project (BOPP) during the second European poverty programme. SPAN is now funded as one of the innovatory initiatives within Poverty 3, and aims to develop and support similar self-help groups of single parents in several other parts of the UK and Europe, some of them in conjunction with the model action projects taking part within Poverty 3. SPAN has raised important questions within the Poverty 3 programme about sexism and racism as key components of the processes of marginalisation and exclusion, and has had some success in getting these issues on the agenda for debate with the other projects, and with the Commission. SPAN has also campaigned for certain principles of good practice within their organisation and within the Poverty 3 programme. These include childcare support and equal representation of Black and White women from SPAN at all Poverty 3 meetings; collective preparation and reporting back from the women who attend meetings on behalf of SPAN; and rotation of representatives from SPAN so that as many women as possible get experience of working at both national and European levels.

FEANTSA is a network of national organisations working with the homeless. It came out of conferences on homelessness in 1985 and 1986, and was formally established in 1989 with funding from the EC. FEANTSA has 20 members, with representatives from all member states except Greece. UK members are Shelter (UK and Scotland) and the Council for the Homeless, Northern Ireland. FEANTSA's major aim is to extend the competence of the EC to include housing. It is arguing for a European housing observatory to be set up with a view to monitoring housing markets, and to integrating national statistics on housing and homelessness, and a budget line (page 23) for research and action projects on housing and homelessness.[39]

There is no overall lobby in the UK for people with disabilities. However, particular organisations and individuals are very active within the Community, for example on the various advisory committees concerned with the HELIOS programme. The National Schizophrenia Fellowship has been active in negotiations with the Commission to try and get mental health projects as well as physical disability projects, included in the HELIOS programme. Within the Commission, UK organisations are generally regarded as well organised and progressive on disability issues, relative to other member states. Disability organisations are now considering how they can best respond to possible future developments at EC level. For example, the RNIB, RNID, the Spastics Society and RADAR are considering resourcing a post in Brussels based at the all-party MEP executive office on disability.

CONCLUSION

It is clear from this chapter that social welfare policy in Europe is in the melting pot, and rapid changes are taking place. In spite of its very limited powers of competence in this field, the Commission is taking an increasing number of social welfare initiatives. Many of these are rather small in scale, and limited in scope. However, they often become the focus for much larger-scale and far-reaching debates. It is almost as if the Commission's tentative moves in the social welfare field are acting as a lightning conductor for the fundamental questions about what kind of welfare state will be constructed at European level, whose values and interests will be served by it, and who will gain and who will lose. There are opportunities for voluntary and community organisations to help shape the outcome of these important debates.

REFERENCES

1   The term 'social protection', as used by the EC, tends to refer to welfare entitlements (like unemployment or sick pay or old age pensions) financed from insurance schemes (from National Insurance in the UK) and paid out to people on the basis of their contributions to the insurance fund. The term 'social assistance' refers to means-tested supplementary welfare benefits, financed from general taxation, and paid out to people on the basis of evidence of need, rather than insurance entitlement.

2   Palmer, *1992 and Beyond*.

3   Abrahamson, P. (1991) *Welfare and Poverty in the Europe of the 1990s: Social Progress or Social Dumping?* Roskilde University, Denmark; Leibfried, S. (1991) *Towards a European Welfare State? On the Integration Potentials of Poverty Regimes in the EC.* Paper to the Anglo-German Conference on Social Justice and Efficiency, University of Nottingham, April; Lister, R. (1990) 'Citizens All?' Inaugural Lecture, University of Bradford, March; Miller, S. M. (1988) The Evolving Welfare State Mixes in Evers, A. and Wintersberger, H. (eds) *Shifts in the Welfare Mix: Their Impact on Work, Social Services and Welfare Policies.* European Centre for Social Welfare Training and Research, Vienna; Offe, C. (1991) *A Non-Productivist Design for Social Policies.* Paper to the Anglo-German Conference on Social Justice and Efficiency, April, University of Nottingham.

4   Berghman, J. (1990) 'The Implications of 1992 for Social Policy: a Selective Critique of Social Insurance Protection' in Mangen et al (eds) *The Implications of 1992 for Social Insurance.* Cross-national research papers, Aston University, Birmingham; Offe, *A Non-Productivist Design for Social Policies.*

5   Townsend, P. (1989) 'And the Walls come Tumbling Down'. *Poverty 75* pp8-11.

6   See Schulte, B. (1990) *National Policies for Social Protection.* Paper to EC conference on poverty and exclusion, October, University of Bath.

7   O'Higgins, M. and Jenkins, S. (1988) *Poverty in Europe*. Available from Centre for the Analysis of Social Policy, University of Bath.

8   Eurostat Rapid Reports (1990) *Inequality and Poverty in Europe 1980-1985*. Available from the Statistical Office of the European Communities, L-2920 Luxembourg.

9   European Observatory on National Family Policies (1990) *Families and Policies: Evolutions and Trends in 1988-1989* CEC DGV. Also available from Institut de l'enfance et de la famille 3 Rue Coq-Heron 75001, Paris.

10   Room, G. and Robbins, D. (1990) *Poverty and Marginalisation in the New Europe: Risks and Insecurities for our Children*. Conference paper. Centre for Research in European Social and Employment Policy, University of Bath.

11   Eurostat (1990) *Rapid Reports: Population and Social Conditions*. CA-NK-90-007-EN-C, Luxembourg.

12   Figures from United Nations (1986) *World Population Prospects*. United Nations, New York.

13   Benington, J. (1991) 'Local Strategies to Combat Poverty: Lessons from the European Programmes', *Critical Public Health* 1 pp23-29; Donnison, D. et al (1991) *Urban Poverty, the Economy and Public Policy: Options for Ireland in the 1990s*. Combat Poverty Agency, Dublin.

14   FEANTSA (1989) *European Action against Homelessness*. First seminar of the European federation of national organisations working with the homeless. FEANTSA, rue Defacq 1, boite 17, 1050 Bruxelles, Belgium.

15   Room and Robbins, *Poverty and Marginalisation* in the New Europe

16   CEC (1991) *Recommendation on Common Criteria Concerning Sufficient Resources and Social Assistance in the Social Protection Systems*. CEC COM(91) 161 final Brussels, 13 May.

17   Abrahamson, *Social Policy in Europe Towards Year 2000*.

18   See CEC (1990) *Social Security for Migrant Workers*. Citizens' Europe Advisory Service, Fact sheet 3. Available from CEC, Citizens' Europe Advisory Service, 8 Storey's Gate, London, SW1 3AT.

19   For further details of the first and second European programme to combat poverty see Room, G. et al (1982) *Europe Against Poverty: The European Poverty Programme 1975-80*, NCVO Publications (incorporating Bedford Square Press)), Room, G. et al (1987) *Action to Combat Poverty: the Experience of 65 Projects*. First report of the programme evaluation team. Centre for the Analysis of Social Policy, University of Bath;

Benington, J. (1990) *The Struggle to Combat Poverty in the UK.* An interim report on 10 UK projects within the second European Programme to Combat Poverty. Local Government Centre working paper, University of Warwick.

20   Townsend, 'And the Walls come Tumbling Down'.

21   Harvey, B. (1990) *Poverty in the European Community.* Extract from final interim report of the European Povisional Working Group Against Poverty. Available from the European Anti-Poverty Network.

22   Further information on this documentation can be obtained from Graham Room, Centre for the Analysis of Social Policy, University of Bath.

23   The observatory on social exclustion is co-ordinated by Graham Room, Centre for the Analysis of Social Policy, University of Bath.

24   Robbins, D. and Room, G. (1991) *Feasibility study report on Marginalisation.* Available from CASP, University of Bath.

25   European Foundation for the Improvement of Living and Working Conditions (1989) *Coping with Social and Economic Change at Neighbourhood Level.* Available from the European Foundation Loughlinstown House, Shankill, County Dublin Ireland.

26   The observatory on elderly people is co-ordinated by Professor Alan Walker at Sheffield University.

27   See 'Action projects slide off EC agenda' in *Eurolink Age Bulletin,* November 1990.

28   For further details, contact HELIOS, 79 avenue de Cortenberg, B-1040 Brussels, Belgium. HELIOS produce a regular newsletter and other useful documentation.

29   This description is taken from Davison and Seary, *Grants from Europe.*

30   *European Information Service* (the bulletin of the Local Government Information Bureau) 115 p44.

31   Further details in Davison and Seary, *Grants from Europe.*

32   Guiglia, A. (1987) *Les 'Sans-Abri' en Europe.* Exchange No 3 January pp3-4. Available from ISG, Barbarossaplatz 2, D-5000 Koln, W Germany.

33   LABOS 1990 *Projet pour la réalisation d'un système d'information européen sur les 'sans-abri.* Rapport final. Available from the European Commission DG V, Brusels; and Drake, 1991 (forthcoming) *Meeting on*

Young Homeless People, Brussels 1989. Conference proceedings. European Commission DG V, Brussels.

34   EAPN can be contacted through the Local Development Unit, National Council for Voluntary Organisations, 26 Bedford Square, London WC1B 3HU.

35   Walker, C. and Walker, A. (1987) *Poverty in Great Britain* National Contextual Paper for the second European Poverty Programme. Available from CASP, University of Bath.

36   Harvey, *Poverty in the European Community*.

37   Wilson, G. (1990) 'Caring and the Welfare State in the 1990s' in Hantrais, L. et al (eds) *Caring and the Welfare State in the 1990s*. Cross-national research papers. University of Aston, Birmingham.

38   Eurolink Age (1990) Age and *Disability: A Challenge for Europe* from Eurolink Age, 1268 London Road, London SW16.

39   FEANTSA (1989) *Memorandum for the meeting of the Housing Minister, Lille, 1989*. Available from FEANTSA (address above).

5

Black and Ethnic Minorities, and Refugees

INTRODUCTION

This chapter begins by looking at how decisions about immigration are taken at a European level, and explores the specific legal disadvantages likely to face people who are not EC nationals in the Europe of 1992. It then discusses the more general problem of racism and discrimination in Europe. Finally it describes what the UK voluntary and community sectors are doing in response to the pressures facing Black and ethnic minorities, migrants and refugees. The particular effects of 1992 on Black and ethnic minority women in the labour market are discussed in Chapter 6.

In the 12 member states of the EC, there are about 15 million people who are Black or from Third World communities. Many of them came to Europe in the 1950s and 1960s in search of work. They helped to rebuild the Europe that had been shattered by the war, and were an important part of the expansionary boom of the 1960s. In Belgium and Germany Moroccans and Turks were recruited to provide cheap and plentiful labour for industry. Other countries used people from former colonies and dependencies, for example people from the Indian subcontinent and the Carribbean in the UK, people from Algeria in France and people from Surinam in the Netherlands. Many of those from former colonies were given the right of settlement but others were not: for example the Turks in Germany were classified as 'guest workers' and it was made extremely difficult for them to gain rights of settlement or security.

The position changed dramatically in the 1970s as the economies of Europe went into recession, although in the UK the position had changed earlier as a result of the 1962 Commonwealth Immigration Act, which ended the right of

Commonwealth citizens to settle in the UK. Barriers to the further inflow of immigrants were made more difficult to penetrate. Now, in the 1990s, the main categories of people migrating to Europe are students, visitors, members of families and asylum seekers. All except asylum seekers are subject to strict rules about maintenance and support before they can enter. This can work harshly against the interests of families, for example, when men working in the UK have to show that they can support dependants wanting to join them.

Asylum seekers have been coming to Europe from many different countries. Some of these have had traditional, often colonial, links with specific European countries, for example Latin America with Spain and Portugal, Angola with Portugal, Ethiopia and Somalia with Italy, Zaire with Belgium, Vietnam with France, and India, Pakistan and Sri Lanka with the UK. Others have created new links, for example the countries of the Middle East (Iran, Iraq and the Lebanon), and parts of Asia.

Most of the discussions about immigration policies at a European level take place outside the framework of the EC. One forum in which they are discussed is the Trevi Group, which comprises the ministers of justice or of the interior or home affairs of each member state. The group was established in 1985 to deal with terrorism, drug-trafficking, illegal immigration and the 'abuse' of asylum by 'bogus refugees'. There is regular input to the meetings from police and security officials. The meetings are held in secret and therefore there is no official record of the group's discussions or decisions.

There is also an Ad Hoc Working Group on Immigration set up on an initiative from the British government and comprising member states' immigration ministers. The European Commission is a member of the Ad Hoc Working Group but does not have membership of the Trevi Group. The Commission is attempting to raise issues concerning 'third country nationals' within the Community institutions. However, it is these two groups that lie outside the Community framework which are attempting to move to a common EC policy on many of the issues affecting Black and ethnic minorities in Europe.[1]

EC INITIATIVES AND THE EFFECTS OF THE SINGLE EUROPEAN MARKET

Three of the key issues facing Black and ethnic minority communities in Europe today, and particularly migrants and refuges, are:

- problems of entry into the area of the Community;

- problems of status once within the Community;

- problems associated with racism and discrimination.

Problems of Entry

The way in which Community immigration policy is likely to develop can be seen from what is known as the Palma Document, drawn up by the group of national co-ordinators appointed by the Ad Hoc Working Group.[2] This document looks at harmonisation in the following areas:

- establishment of a common list of countries whose citizens are subject to a visa requirement;

- establishment of a common list of persons to be refused entry;

- introduction of a European visa;

- acceptance of identical international commitments with regard to asylum;

- a method of determining the state responsible for examining the application for asylum and conditions governing the movement of the applicant between member states.

These measures will make it more difficult for potential immigrants and asylum seekers to gain entry to the EC. There will be a greater requirement for visas, and once one EC country has refused an application for asylum or residence, it will not be legal to try other EC countries. Naturally, the fears of voluntary and pressure groups working on these issues is that future EC policy will be based on the practices and requirements of the most restrictive member state.

The first moves towards putting some of these policies into practice were taken in 1985 when five countries, France, West Germany, Belgium, Luxembourg and the Netherlands, signed a formal agreement in Schengen in Luxembourg to abolish their internal border controls ahead of the rest of the EC, known as the 'Schengen Convention'. Italy, Spain and Portugal are likely to sign the agreement in the future. The Schengen Convention covers a number of issues that have been referred to above.[3] There will be increased policing of external borders, and citizens of non-EC countries will be subject to particularly stringent checks. A uniform visa will be introduced. There will be a 'one-chance-only' rule for asylum seekers. Cross-border surveillance and 'hot pursuit' across borders will be allowed in certain circumstances. There will be a computerised information system on wanted or missing persons and on people to be refused admittance at EC borders. In 1991 however, following intensive lobbying by Dutch non-government organisations, the Dutch State Council ruled that the Netherlands could not implement the Schengen Convention because of prior international obligations. This may lead to modifications of the Convention. All member states have now also agreed a new convention which contains complicated rules for determining which member state is responsible for processing individual requests for asylum.

The net result of these developments has been described as meaning a 'bleak outlook' for refugees.[4] Some commentators now refer to the EC as 'Fortress Europe', implying that as internal barriers come down and ultimately disappear the external barriers will become much more important, and will aim to keep out non-EC nationals, particularly those from the Third World.

The attitude of the British government has been to support the initiatives outlined in the Palma Document, referred to above. However, it does not want to abolish internal border controls for those people coming from another country within the EC. The British government has continued to insist on passport and document checks at the point of entry to the UK. In 1989 Mrs Thatcher was quoted as saying:

> we joined Europe to have free movement of goods... I did not join Europe to have free movement of terrorists, criminals, drugs, plant and animal diseases and rabies, and illegal immigrants. How are you going to stop anyone from Bangladesh, from any country, coming for a holiday in Greece, coming right in, right across all borders, no controls, and settling in Britain and we would have no means of finding out?[5]

Problems of Status

One consequence of any significant relaxation of frontier controls between member states will be a greater reliance on internal immigration controls. This is already the case in many of the member states. Examples of such increased controls could be greater powers for the police to stop and question people, and the enforcement of workplace controls requiring employers to check the immigration status of anyone applying for work. The debate about such increased controls includes the question of a compulsory identity card.

One of the declared aims of the removal of internal barriers is to create freedom of movement within the Community so that there is no discrimination for workers based on nationality. However, this freedom will only be available to nationals of the 12 member states, i.e. to full citizens. So EC nationals will have greatly superior rights to non-EC nationals living and working in the Community.[6] EC nationals will not only have the right to work in other countries, but will also have extensive protection against discrimination under Community law, and will receive various other benefits, including mutual recognition of qualifications, protection under labour laws, entitlement to local rates of social security and other benefits, and free education for children. There have been proposals from the Commission that legally established migrant workers should have improved rights and guarantees in these areas, including the right to vote in local elections. However, for the immediate future migrant workers will be governed only by the national laws of the country in which they are living. In many cases this will relegate them to second class status with reduced rights in areas such as protection from discrimination and access to social security, health and welfare benefits.[7]

Problems Associated with Racism and Discrimination

Several voluntary and community organisations and other commentators have also expressed concern about what many perceive to be a growth in racism throughout the EC.[8] There is evidence of increased racial attacks against minorities in most of the member states, and an increase in the number of fascist and extreme right wing candidates elected to local and national governments. In mid-1991, such MEPs held 21 seats in the European Parliament.

In 1986 the European Parliament approved a report of a parliamentary committee on the rise of fascism and racism in Europe.[9] One of the report's recommendations was that the Community institutions should make a joint declaration against racism and xenophobia. A declaration, agreed in June 1988, expressed a determination to protect 'the individuality and dignity of every member of society'. However, when the Commission made further proposals to the Council of Ministers in May 1990 to reinforce the original declaration, the Council watered-down the proposed recommendations, deleting reference to third-country nationals and to possible Community action in this area. This resulted in the Commissioner for Social Affairs and Employment withdrawing the Commission's support for the final agreed statement, because it did not go far enough. In particular, the Commission regretted the Council's deletion of 'reference to possible Community action in this area'.[10]

In 1989 the European Parliament established a second committee on racism in Europe, which produced a number of recommendations including:

- voting rights in local elections for immigrants with five years' EC residence;

- a European resident's card allowing immigrants to work and travel in the EC;

- measures to allow immigrants to achieve full nationality after five years' residence;

- harmonised anti-discriminatory legislation;

- a budget for anti-racist projects;

- an end to secrecy in the way that decisions are made in this area;

- a European 'Year of Racial Harmony' in 1995.

However, this report ran into much opposition in the European Parliament, not just from right-wing MEPs, but from centre and left MEPs worried about the consequences of being seen to support such proposals. This reflects the difficulties of getting issues to do with race and immigration discussed within the Community institutions. There is as yet no legal basis for doing so in the way that there is a legal basis for equal opportunities legislation in the area of discrimination against women.

THE ROLE OF THE VOLUNTARY AND COMMUNITY SECTORS

In the UK there are several well-established groups campaigning on issues relevant to refugees, asylum seekers and the rights of migrants. The Refugee Council has produced a manifesto supported by over 70 different organisations.[11] Point 9 of this manifesto states that every refugee in the EC should enjoy the same rights of movement, work, political, social and religious activity as EC nationals. Point 10 asks national governments and the EC to help long-term settlement by funding refugee community groups and agencies working with refugees. The Refugee Council has also been involved in the establishment of the European Consultation on Refugees and Exiles (ECRE), which takes up these issues at the European level with interested groups from the other member states.[12]

The Refugee Forum has produced a Refugee Charter for Europe. This has similar objectives to the Refugee Manifesto and covers much of the same ground. In addition, the Refugee Forum, with the Migrants Rights Action Network, has produced a European Migrant and Refugee Manifesto with ten demands including rights to stay, to family reunion, to free movement, and full social, political rights and legal rights.

Liberty (formerly the National Council for Civil Liberties) has produced a leaflet on its concerns about the effects of 1992, including its concern about the threat of Fortress Europe.[13] It outlines three areas where it would like to see change. Firstly, it wants EC refugee policies to be consistent with the Geneva Convention. Secondly, it wants racial discrimination to be outlawed in all areas, particularly where it restricts freedom of movement. And thirdly, it emphasises that the fundamental principle must be equal rights without discrimination, i.e. that EC benefits should apply equally to EC nationals and residents, including voting rights which should be extended to all EC residents, irrespective of nationality.

While there has been considerable activity around the concerns of refugees and migrants and the rights of resident non-nationals, there has been less activity so far on the issue of racism and discrimination. In some ways the UK is the most advanced of the 12 member states on this front. For example, it is the only country in the Community whose legislation covers discrimination on the grounds of race. However, there is still a great deal of concern about the situation in the UK and about preserving those gains that have been made.

A recent development has been the establishment of SCORE (the Standing Conference on Racial Equality in Europe). This body emerged from a conference organised by the Commission for Racial Equality to discuss the position in Europe and the likely effects of 1992. An independent steering group was established which led to a founding conference in late 1990. SCORE hopes to make links with similar groups in other member states. Its aims are to:

- co-operate in the exchange and dissemination of information;

- work for the equality of condition of all those resident in the Community;

- promote legislation and action that will ensure equal treatment for Black and migrant communities and outlaw discrimination;

- promote legislation that will outlaw harassment and incitement to racial hatred or violence.[14]

CONCLUSION

The year 1992 is likely to exacerbate the problems facing Black and ethnic minorities and refugees in the EC. However, there are immense difficulties in raising issues in this area at a European level. The issues are not recognised in the treaties governing the operations of the Community. Indeed many of the decisions taken at European level (and these are increasing) are not taken within the framework of the Community but in the secret meetings of the

Trevi Group and the Ad Hoc Working Group on Immigration. There are some indications that the Commission wishes to change this. The Commission has also sponsored the Migrant's Forum, as a mechanism for consulting groups concerned with the rights of migrants. This illustrates its willingness to initiate a more direct dialogue with migrant communities independently of its negotiations with national governments. Furthermore, recent expressions of anti-semitic feeling in the inner-city areas of France and Belgium may bring pressure for more anti-racist action. There may not be a clear legal mandate for Community competence in this area but there is still a great deal for voluntary organisations to campaign for, in ensuring that the issues are put on the agenda, and that the appropriate debates take place in an open forum.

REFERENCES

1   Gordon, P. (1989) *Fortress Europe? The Meaning of 1992.* The Runnymede Trust, 11 Princelet Street, London E1 6QH.

2   Spencer, M. (1990) *1992 and All That: Civil Liberties in the Balance.* Civil Liberties Trust, 21 Tabard Street, London SE1 4LA.

3   Joint Council for the Welfare of Immigrants (1989) *Unequal Migrants: The European Community's Unequal Treatment of Migrants and Refugees.* Policy Papers in Ethnic Relations, 13, JCWI and Centre for Research in Ethnic Relations, Warwick University.

4   Spencer, *1992 and All That.*

5   Quoted in *The Daily Mail*, 18 May 1989.

6   Joint Council for the Welfare of Immigrants *Unequal Migrants.*

7   Spencer, *1992 and All That.*

8   Dummett, A. (1990) *Europe and 1992 Focus on Racial Issues.* Catholic Association for Racial Justice, St Vincent's Centre, Talma Road, London SW2 1AS; Gordon, *Fortress Europe?*

9   European Parliament (1985) *Committee of Inquiry into the Rise of Fascism and Racism in Europe.* Report on the findings of the inquiry.

10   Quoted in *The European Citizen*, 2 July/August 1990.

11   Refugee Council *Refugee Manifesto*, available from the Refugee Council, Broadway House, 3/9 Broadway, London, SW8 15J.

12   Rudge, P. (1989) *Into the 1990s: The Outlook for Refugees*. Speech given at AGM of the Refugee Council 1989.

13   Liberty (1990) *1992 and You: Fighting for Your Rights!*. Liberty, 21 Tabard Street, London SE1 4LA.

14   SCORE can be contacted through the Greater London Action for Racial Equality, St Margaret's House, 21 Old Ford Road, London, E2 9PL.

6

Women

INTRODUCTION

This chapter looks at some of the issues which are of significance to women and women's organisations in the EC. The emphasis is primarily on women's relationship to the labour market, reflecting the employment focus of the Treaty of Rome and the SEA, and thus the dominant theme of most people's thinking about the implications of 1992 for women. However, this chapter also includes a discussion of childcare issues in the context of 1992. It begins by identifying relevant demographic trends and some features of the female labour market in the EC.

Demographic Trends and Features of the Female Labour Market

Over the next 20 years or so, an important trend in the European labour market will be a shortage of labour, mainly as a result of the contraction in the size of the 16-24 age group due to demographic changes (this is referred to as the 'numbers gap' by Rajan in Chapter 3, page 56). One way of meeting this labour shortage will be for employers and policy makers to encourage more women to participate in the labour market. A noticeable feature of the last few decades in any case has been the arrival of large numbers of women on the labour market, primarily due to younger generations of women with different marriage, childbearing and working patterns from previous generations, but demographic trends will now greatly strengthen this pattern. It is anticipated that during the 1990s most labour force growth will be accounted for by women.[1]

Women are still, however, less likely to be economically active than men. The 1986 European labour market survey showed that 79 per cent of men in the 14-65 age group were economically active compared to only 49 per cent of women.[2] Research has suggested that the major barrier to increased labour force participation rates among women is the lack of suitable childcare arrangements for children aged 0-10,[3] and this has led the Commission to attach great importance to childcare as an equality issue.[4] In the UK there are signs that more and more policy-makers and employers now recognise the direct link between women's economic activity rates and levels of childcare provision, and the need to combine labour market policies with childcare policies.[5]

A significant proportion of the Community's workforce is employed in what the Commission calls 'atypical' forms of work (part-time and temporary work, homeworking, sub-contracting, etc.), and women make up the majority of these 'atypical' workers. This means that women bear the brunt of the relatively poor conditions of employment attached to 'atypical' work. In Britain, over 80 per cent of part-time employees are women workers, and they constitute some 42 per cent of all women employees.[6] It is important to note that this form of employment is frequently an involuntary option for both men and women.[7]

Paradoxically, there has been an increase in both employment and unemployment rates among women in the EC.[8] This has happened because jobs have not necessarily been in the right place or the right sector, and because there have not been enough opportunities to satisfy the needs of the increasing number of women entering the labour market and the existing number of women unemployed.[9] Unemployment data broken down by gender show that female unemployment rates in the EC are always and everywhere higher than male rates, with the exception of British and Irish figures for under-25 unemployment.[10] Furthermore, because many women are not formally categorised as unemployed, rates of unemployment among women are likely to be underestimates.

Finally, it is important to note the continuing discrepancy between male and female rates of pay in the EC. Despite equal pay legislation (page 107) the gap between the wages paid to men and those paid to women remain significant in most parts of the Community. It has been estimated that the average earnings of women in the EC are 31 per cent less than those of men.[11] This, together with the increased numbers of single-parent families, the majority of which are headed by women, and the increased numbers of elderly people, mostly women, means that a significant majority of the European poor are women.[12]

THE EFFECTS OF THE SINGLE EUROPEAN MARKET

In a booklet published as part of a series on the implications of 1992 for social policy, Finch suggests that '...the creation of a single market in the EC appears more likely to make matters worse rather than better from the perspective of equal opportunities and women's rights'.[13]

The primary reason given for this assertion is the already marginal position of much women's work in the labour market and the possibility that women will be more marginalised post-1992. A central theme of the SEA is that it should create a more flexible workforce, with fewer people working as employees in permanent, fixed jobs and more working in positions which are temporary, with fixed term contracts, in part-time work or as self-employed.[14] It is likely that the successful creation of this more flexible labour market will therefore push women 'even further away from equal access to secure jobs with good rewards'.[15] A New Statesman Society article has concluded:

> The deregulation of labour markets - spearheaded by the Thatcher government - has already set in motion a downward spiral of deteriorating working conditions and increasing insecurity, gathering momentum as 1992 approaches. And women are likely to be the main victims.[16]

There are three further reasons why women are likely to be particularly vulnerable to the implementation of the single market. Firstly, 9 out of the 40 industries identified by the Commission as particularly sensitive to single European market changes (Table 2, page 51) have over 45 per cent women employees, and in a further nine of the vulnerable industries women represent between 30 per cent and 45 per cent of employees.[17] Secondly, the increased competition created by the single market is likely to result in reduced demand for jobs requiring few qualifications - i.e. primarily women's jobs. And thirdly, free movement of labour will be more likely to discriminate against women than men. It will be harder for women, who have the main responsibility for caring for others, to move around the Community for work or for training,[18] and they may be particularly affected by variations in social security provisions between countries. For instance, a woman working in France may not be able to claim her rights to the high levels of maternity provision or child care in that country if she chooses to work in the UK.[19]

A preliminary study on the impact of 1992 on Black and ethnic minority women in the UK has revealed that they may be particularly disadvantaged by the introduction of the single European market.[20] For example, Black and ethnic minority women are disproportionately represented among 'atypical' employees (the National Homeworking Unit estimates that more than 50 per cent of UK homeworkers are Black and ethnic minority women), and are also disproportionately concentrated in some of the 1992 sensitive industries identified in Table 2 (page 51), particularly the textile, electrical engineering and electronics industries.

On a more positive note, it is suggested that the publicity surrounding the completion of the single market by 1992, together with the publication of European 'league tables' showing the UK's poor record on childcare, has alerted some employers to the additional problems they may face in recruiting within a European labour market if they do not take on board the need for more childcare provision.[21] 1992 could therefore provide an impetus for improved childcare facilities within the UK.

The focus on women and 1992 has primarily been in terms of women's relationship to the labour market, and the associated issue of childcare for working parents. However, many women are not part of the paid workforce. It has been suggested that the SEA and the Social Charter could increase the likelihood of *employment* becoming the main basis for welfare entitlements rather than *citizenship*, and in some countries this could result in a worsening of social rights for women outside the labour market. The UK welfare state has traditionally emphasised the social rights of citizens, albeit partially, as well as those of employees, but Finch argues that as we increasingly enter a European context this could change, and may result in women being doubly disadvantaged: '[women] will lack the rewards which are derived from receiving good wages or salaries on a secure and predictable basis, and they will also be denied access to good pensions, health care and whatever other benefits are going to accrue to securely employed individuals in member states'.[22]

EC INITIATIVES

Article 119 of the Treaty of Rome states that 'each member state shall ... ensure and maintain the principle that men and women shall receive equal pay for equal work'. The original aim of this article was to encourage free competition between employers by avoiding any distortion of the market through the use of lower-paid female workers. It therefore reflects the essentially economic concerns of the EC, rather than any general recognition of the need for equality in its own right. However, Article 119 has provided a useful basis for Community action in favour of (working) women and particularly for the development of equal opportunities legislation. This activity is overseen by the Equal Opportunities Office of the Commission, and the Women's Rights

Committee of the European Parliament,[23] with input from the Advisory Committee on Equal Opportunities (made up of two representatives from each member state - the chair and deputy chair of the Equal Opportunities Commission in the case of the UK), and most recently the European Women's Lobby (page 110).

Whitting argues that, from the perspective of UK women, EC involvement in equal opportunities has appeared particularly attractive because of the low priority the issue has been given in contemporary British politics.[24] And, the National Alliance of Women's Organisations (NAWO) suggests that 'although the UK government has been notoriously unenthusiastic in embracing European legislation, membership of the EC has undoubtedly been a positive experience for British women'.[25]

EC initiatives in the area of equal opportunities for women fall into two categories: legislation and action programmes. The rest of this section describes the key initiatives in each category.

Legislation

Since 1975 there have been five major directives which have improved equality for women.[26] The first **directive on equal pay** in 1975 extended Article 119 by introducing the concept of work of equal value and included conditions of work. It abolished any discriminatory clauses in collective agreements and provided protection for employees for dismissal following complaints. Although an important landmark, the Local Government International Bureau has suggested that 'one of the EC's least successful directives is that establishing the principle of equal opportunities for men and women. 15 years after the adoption of the directive, the Commission has just sent its third action programme to assist its implementation to the Council of Ministers'.[27]

The **directive on equal treatment** in 1976 dealt with women's *access* to employment, training, promotion and working conditions, and has resulted in it no longer being legal for a woman employed by a public body to be forced to retire before a man. The 1979 **directive on equal treatment in social security** covered statutory social security schemes giving protection against risks of sickness, invalidity, accidents at work, occupational diseases and unemployment. It applied only to the working population and did not cover retirement ages. This directive led eventually in 1987 to the payment of the Invalidity Care Allowance to married women in the UK. The 1986 **directive on occupational social security schemes** covered all schemes, whether optional or compulsory, that provide employees or self-employed people with benefits intended to replace state schemes. It also outlaws direct or indirect discrimination on the basis of sex or marital or family status. Finally, the 1986 **self-employed directive** was introduced to ensure equal treatment between self-employed men and women, including those in agriculture.

In addition, there are a number of draft directives which have so far been blocked but are still officially 'on the table'. The one receiving much publicity at the time of writing is that containing the Commission's proposals to extend the rights and protections of full-time workers to **part-time and temporary workers**. Given that the majority of 'atypical' workers are women, this directive would help considerably in reducing continued discrimination against women in the workplace. Conroy Jackson suggests 'Additional social protection for the holders of atypical employment contracts is socially just and would benefit women. But it is more than that. It is a buffer against the use of secondary and unregulated labour markets as a competitive edge in a unified Europe where monopolies will play a greater role.'[28] The British government is one of the main opponents of the draft directive. It has argued that the measures are 'unnecessary and misguided' and seem 'deliberately designed to discriminate against part-time work'.[29]

Since 1983 there has also been a draft directive on **parental and family leave**, which would give three months' leave to either parent after maternity leave and before the child was two years old. The UK is the only member state to offer no statutory form of parental leave. In 1987 the Commission proposed a directive on **maternity rights and provisions**, which would harmonise and protect the employment rights of pregnant women. This again would benefit UK women because the UK is the only member state whose maternity provision has worsened in the 1980s. In October 1987 the Commission proposed a directive **completing the implementation of the principle of equal treatment for men and women in statutory and occupational social security schemes**, and in July 1988 on **burden of proof in the law of member states of the EC**, which would put the burden of proof on employers in equality cases.

Action Programmes

To date there have been two EC action programmes on equal opportunties for women, from 1982-1985 and 1986-1990, which have included Commission support of a range of measures to combat female unemployment, and to encourage equal opportunities at all levels of education and training. Particular priority has been given to women disadvantaged in the labour market, including single parents or women from ethnic minorities or with disabilities. One example of support is the start-up grants the Commission has made available to women's local employment initiatives, covering both small businesses and not-for-profit initiatives. In addition, a number of women's training programmes and workshops have been funded through the

ESF. One such initiative is the South Glamorgan Women's Training Workshop, which trains economically and socially disadvantaged women in computing and micro-electronics and provides on-site childcare for trainees' children.[30] Finally, a number of networks have been established, including the IRIS network on vocational training for women (Box L), and the Childcare Network. The latter was established in 1986 and consists of an expert from each member state and a co-ordinator.[31] It conducts reviews of childcare services and policies throughout the Community and makes recommendations for action by the Commission, member states and social partners.[32]

BOX L

THE IRIS NETWORK

Now in its third year of operation, the IRIS network offers a wide variety of services and activities promoting women's training and building links between women's training programmes.

The European Commission finances the IRIS network and has overall responsibility for it. The Centre for Research on European Women (CREW) is an independent organisation responsible for the general co-ordination of IRIS and the everyday management of its work.

IRIS offers:

- contacts with other women's training programmes throughout the EC;

- possibilities for transnational partnerships and exchanges;

- publicity grants for model programmes;

- the IRIS database of women's training programmes, technical national evaluation meetings and more broad-based seminars on women's training needs;

- IRIS publications including the IRIS bulletin with up-to-date news on training and on the network and IRIS conference dossiers;

- the IRIS directory giving an updated profile of network members;

- a computerised electronic mail and bulletin board.

Further information on the IRIS network can be obtained from CREW, 38 Rue Stevin, 1040 Brussels.

Source: IRIS infomation bulletin, available from CREW

A third action programme[33] was announced in late 1990 (amid rumours that the draft proposal has been watered down by some in the Commission). The main thrust of this programme will be to ensure member states' greater compliance with the equal opportunties directives of the last 15 years to try and achieve the aim of women's equality now enshrined within the Social Charter (Box C, page 19), and to direct more money from the Structural Funds to fund new schemes that promote vocational training for women. This will be achieved through the NOW initiative (New Opportunities for Women, described in Box G, page 61).

THE ROLE OF THE VOLUNTARY AND COMMUNITY SECTORS

Historically, women's organisations have shown a fair degree of ambivalence towards involvement in the EC. For some women the European institutions are another product of male power structures, and the single market is seen primarily as being about 'business men in suits'. However, many women are increasingly recognising the potential benefits of EC involvement in equal opportunities issues, and are becoming involved in European activities.

Hoskyns[34] describes how the European Network of Women (ENOW), launched in 1983, was the first example of feminist women identifying a need to 'enter the mainstream' of European politics. During the 1980s ENOW[35] made links between grassroots women's organisations and European institutions, initiating action on issues affecting women at a European level. It campaigned for more recognition in the second European anti-poverty programme of the particular disadvantage suffered by women, pointing out that although each of the programme's theme groups (elderly, long-term unemployed, etc.) contained a high percentage of women, the Commission had failed to identify women as a priority category. Some commentators have suggested that the design of Poverty 3 (page 80) has done nothing to redress this shortcoming of the earlier programme, and even further conceals women as a major group in poverty. In 1988 ENOW was awarded a small EC grant to hold a tribunal on women and poverty in Brussels.

Towards the end of 1990, the European Women's Lobby (EWL) was formally launched, and this now provides an important focus for women's organisations developing a European dimension to their work.[36] Much of its work centres on the third equal opportunites action programme. The Lobby also proposes to conduct research and action on the feminisation of poverty in the EC and on the effects on Black, migrant and ethnic minority women of the increasing co-ordination of immigration procedures in the EC member states.

Hoskyns has suggested that there are two key questions facing the EWL in the early stages of its development: 'the first is: can the Lobby become sufficiently expert and competent, and well-enough resourced, to have a real impact in the Brussels jungle? The second is: can the Lobby be sufficiently broad-based, democratic and accountable (and well-enough resourced) to justify its claims to represent women across the EC?'.[37] Despite these difficult challenges facing the EWL, Hoskyns notes that it is exciting that at a time when similar structures for women hardly exist at the national level, women are seeking to establish participatory and effective transnational mechanisms at a European level.

The National Alliance of Women's Organisations has also been active, along with other voluntary organisations, in responding to the draft directives on protection at work of pregnant women, and on part-time and temporary work.[38] The National Federation of Women's Institutes (NFWI) is increasingly adding a European dimension to its work: for example by monitoring European policies of relevance to rural areas, by active involvement in the work and policy documents of COFACE[39] (the European network of family organisations), and most recently by involvement in the EWL. Other women's organisations are campaigning on women's training issues, particularly those involved in the European networks such as IRIS (Box L). Many of the major UK childcare organisations are involved with a campaigning group 'Childcare Now', which focuses on lobbying for European models of publicly-funded childcare to be adopted in the UK, and lends support to the recommendations of the European Childcare Network.[40]

CONCLUSION

The single European market is likely to bring both opportunities and dangers for women in Europe. As Whitting suggests, 1992 offers an occasion to raise and resolve issues that effect women's employment opportunities and outcomes. And, it is likely to provide an additional impetus for improved childcare facilities within the UK. However, 1992 may 'reinforce rather than reduce the precarious and exploitative situation that typifies women's employment in member state countries',[41] and is likely to hold particular risks for poor women and those from Black and ethnic minorities. Finally, there are dangers that the needs of women *outside* the labour market will be neglected, if as has been predicted, 1992 results in social rights becoming increasingly focused around employment rather than citizenship.

REFERENCES

1   Department of Employment, Factsheet 2 quoted in Hughes, J. and Simpson, R. (1990) 'The Ghost Without Hamlet?' Social rights for part-time workers in Europe *Poverty* 77 pp 10-13.

2   Quoted in Crawley, C. (1990) 1992 and its effects on women. *European Labour Forum*. 2 Autumn pp44-46.

3   Moss, P. and Phillips, A. (1989) *Who Cares for Europe's Children?* CEC Luxembourg.

4   Moss, P. (1990) *Childcare in the European Communities 1985-1990*. Women of Europe supplement 31, CEC Brussels.

5   Cohen, B. (1990) *Caring for Children: the 1990 Report*. Report for the European Commission's Childcare Network on childcare services and policy in the UK. Family Policy Studies Centre.

6   Hughes and Simpson, 'The Ghost without Hamlet?'

7   Meulders, D. and Plasman, R. (1989) *Women in Atypical Employment*. Final Report CEC, Brussels

8   CEC (1987) *Equal Opportunities for Women*. European File 10/87 CC-AD-87-010-EN-C.

9   Conroy Jackson, P. (1990) *The Impact of the Completion of the Internal Market on Women in the European Community*. Prepared for the Equal Opportunities Unit of DGV of the EC V/506/90/EN.

10   Conroy Jackson, P. *The Impact of the Completion of the Internal Market on Women in the European Community*.

11   Conroy Jackson, P. *The Impact of the Completion of the Internal Market on Women in the European Community*.

12   Daly, M. (1990) *Women and Poverty*. Attic Press, Dublin.

13   Finch, J. (1990) 'Women, Equal Opportunities and Welfare in the European Community: Some Questions and Issues' in (eds) O'Brien, M., Hantrais, L., and Mangen, S. *Women, Equal Opportunities and Welfare*. Cross National Research Papers, Aston University, Birmingham.

14   Whitting, G. (1990) 'Women and 1992: Opportunity or Disaster?' in Manning, N. and Ungerson, C. (eds) *Social Policy Review*, Longman, London.

15   Finch, 'Women, Equal Opportunities and Welfare in the European Community'.

16   Huws, U. (1989) 'Danger: Women at Work' *New Statesman, Society* 12 March pp 12-13.

17   Conroy Jackson, *The Impact of the Completion of the Internal Market on Women in the European Community.*

18   Crawley, '1992 and its Effects on Women'.

19   Pillinger, J. (1991) 'The Single European Market and Women' *Local Work* monthly bulletin of the Centre for Local Economic Strategies (CLES), Alberton House, St Mary's Parsonage, Manchester M3 2WJ.

20   Goldsmith, J. (1990) *Summary of Preliminary Study of the Impact of the Creation of the 1992 Single European Market on Black and Ethnic Minority Women in the UK.* National Alliance of Women's Organisations, 279-281 Whitechapel Road, London, E1 1BY.

21   Cohen, *Caring for Children.*

22   Finch, 'Women, Equal Opportunities and Welfare in the European Community'.

23   Crawley, C. (1990) 'The European Parliament Committee on Women's Rights' in (eds) O'Brien, M., Hantrais, L., and Mangen, S. *Women, Equal Opportunities and Welfare.* Cross National Research Papers, Aston University, Birmingham.

24   Whitting, 'Women and 1992: Opportunity or Disaster?'

25   Grant, J. (1990) *1992: Women and Europe. Opportunities and Dangers.* National Alliance of Women's Organisations.

26   The description of EC legislation is taken from Grant, 1992: *Women and Europe.*

27   Quoted in the European Information Service (a monthly bulletin produced by the Local Government International Bureau, see Appendix E for further details on this bulletin) 115 p23.

28   Conroy Jackson, *The Impact of the Completion of the Internal Market on Women in the European Community.*

29   Quoted in Hughes and Simpson, 'The Ghost Without Hamlet?'

30   Essex, S. et al (1986) *New Styles of Training for Women.* An evaluation of South Glamorgan Women's Workshop. Equal Opportunities Commission.

31   The co-ordinator of the Childcare network is Peter Moss, Thomas Coram Research Unit, 41 Brunswick Square, London, WC1N 1AZ. The UK national expert is Bronwen Cohen, SCAFA, 55 Albany Street, Edinburgh EH1 3QY.

32   Moss, *Childcare in the European Communities 1985-1990*; Cohen, Caring for Children.

33   CEC (1990) *Equal Opportunities for Men and Women: Third Action Programme*. Background Report. November ISEC/B33/90.

34   Hoskyns, 'The European Women's Lobby'.

35   European Network on Women (ENOW) UK office: 52/54 Featherstone Street, London WC1 8RT.

36   For an account of the historical development of the European Women's Lobby see Grant, 1992: *Women and Europe*; Hoskyns, 'The European Women's Lobby'.

37   Hoskyns 'The European Women's Lobby'.

38   NAWO (1990a) *Response to the Employment Department Consultative Document on the European Commission's Draft Directives on Part-time and Temporary Work and Working Time*. NAWO, London; NAWO (1990b) *Response on the Proposed EC Directive on Protection at Work of Pregnant Women or Those who have recently given Birth* NAWO, London.

39   COFACE's office is at Rue de Londres 17, 1050 Brussels, Belgium.

40   For details, see Cohen, *Caring for Children*.

41   Whitting, 'Women and 1992: Opportunity or Disaster?'

7

Health

INTRODUCTION

This chapter discusses some of the ways in which EC activities impinge upon, and may in the future affect, health issues in the UK. The primary focus is on how 1992 might affect the public and occupational health spheres, rather than health-care systems. Other health issues are covered in previous chapters of this report: groups concerned with the health and caring of disabled and elderly people will find useful material in Chapter 4, and environmental health issues are discussed in Chapter 8. The health of populations is of course also affected by many of the broader socio-economic policies discussed in this report.

Health policy is generally described as lying outside the boundaries of EC competence, with the important exception of occupational health. However, many organisations are becoming increasingly aware of the extent to which the public health is affected by wider EC decision-making, concerning, for example, the CAP or taxation policies. Furthermore, there are several examples where, notwithstanding limited competence, the EC has forayed into the health field. This is partly because certain health-oriented activities are able to attract popular, and thus political, support with relative ease, and are therefore areas where EC action has been possible, however tenuous the legal base. Such activities often have had the additional bonus of bolstering the human-face of Community activity.

EC INITIATIVES AND THE EFFECTS OF THE SINGLE EUROPEAN MARKET

Health-Care Systems

To date, membership of the EC has not had any significant impact on the development of UK policy and practice on health-care, nor upon the NHS. Gough and Edwards argue that health and social security 'are major policy domains where the autonomy of the nation state has hardly yet been ruffled'.[1] However, McCarthy has suggested that, in the longer term, the 1992 project could result in market principles exerting an increasing influence on health-care systems in Europe, and ultimately could have major implications for the NHS:

> In the UK, EC directives for free trade could increase pressure to deregulate the existing state monopoly. Although supplementary private health insurance is readily available in this country, free traders could argue that individuals could be allowed a choice of basic insurance, and that private insurers from other EC countries should have the same access to health insurance markets as the state does. Mixed public and private health insurance exists in other EC countries, and appears to be as acceptable to their citizens as the NHS is to ours. But a move to private insurance for basic medical care would abandon one of the fundamental principles of the National Health Service.[2]

If further deregulation of the state health sector was to occur, it would of course be extremely difficult to distinguish the part played by greater European integration, from that arising from the current NHS reorganisation and newly created internal markets within health care.

Health and Safety at Work

It is estimated that one-quarter to one-third of the social class variation in health in the UK is due to occupational factors.[3] Occupational health measures may be extremely important, therefore, in reducing the growing social-class health inequalities in this country. The SEA considerably strengthens the powers of the EC in the area of occupational health and safety. USDAW (Union of Shop, Distributive and Allied Workers) report that it is now the EC rather than the British government that has the major responsibility for introducing new health and safety laws.[4] Unlike many of the other areas in the Social Charter, most of the declarations on health and safety at work in the Charter have been endorsed by the British government. Furthermore, the UK Health and Safety Commission has clearly acknowledged the shift of decision-making from the national to the EC level:

> We propose to recognise that henceforth the European programme will represent the overwhelming share of our legislative effort. We shall pursue domestic legislative projects only where they are particularly important... and where there is not an early or obvious place for them in the European programme.[5]

In 1988 the EC made proposals for a package of six new directives on health and safety at work. Four have so far been adopted and must be implemented by December 1992. The most important is called the 'Framework Directive', which lays down the ground rules on health and safety by setting out employers' responsibilities and workers' rights. Every employer will have the duty to ensure the health and safety of workers. This will include assessing and avoiding risks, introducing preventive measures, using specialist health and safety advice, monitoring potential hazards, and keeping records on certain accidents and diseases. Employers will also have to provide information, safety training, and agree consultation procedures with the workforce. The other directives include the safety requirements for VDU operators, and workers' rights to training and consultation on the introduction of VDUs.[6] Finally, 1992 has been designated the 'European Year of Health and Safety'.

Tobacco Policy

As part of the proposals to harmonise tax levels in the single market, the EC has proposed a directive to set minimum and maximum rates of tax on tobacco and alcohol throughout the Community.[7] This would have the effect of raising taxes in some countries, for example, the Mediterranean countries, and of lowering them in others. The UK currently levies one of the higher rates of excise duty upon alcohol and tobacco, and therefore if such a proposal were implemented, UK cigarette and alcohol prices would be expected to fall. The British and some other governments have opposed this proposal, which requires unanimous approval. Research indicates that consumption levels are clearly linked to price and so anti-smoking pressure groups are also opposed to the lowering of prices. More recently, the introduction of tax bands has been proposed, which would allow more flexibility and might prevent a fall in the price of cigarettes in the UK.

A directive on the labelling of tobacco products was adopted at the EC Council of Health Ministers in 1989. This provides for standardised health

117

warnings to be printed on cigarette packets, and on other tobacco products from January 1992. The British government abstained in the vote on the adoption of this directive, preferring to maintain the voluntary agreement currently in operation in this country, but in this instance only a qualified majority vote was required, and so the directive was passed. This will mean that 'tobacco seriously damages health' will appear on the front of all cigarette packets and tobacco product packaging in the UK, and the back will bear one of six warnings, including the strong message 'smoking kills'. The British government is also opposing any further restrictions on advertising and sponsorship, and thus is hostile, with Denmark, Germany and the Netherlands, to the proposed directive to ban all tobacco advertising and promotion.[8] A tar-yield directive was adopted in 1990 and a resolution restricting smoking in public places was passed in 1989.[9]

Nutrition Policy

The completion of a single European market by the end of 1992 has provided the impetus for European legislation on a variety of aspects of food production, including food labelling and declaration of additives. The new European labelling system will be voluntary, as is presently the case with the UK system. However, it is the responsibility of the Commission to monitor and review the operation of this directive. If, as seems likely, few food manufacturers opt into the voluntary system, more serious consideration may be given to compulsory nutrition labelling in the future. A proposal is also being developed to control the health claims which manufacturers and advertisers make about food on their products.[10]

In December 1990 the EC health ministers endorsed a proposal to initiate an action programme on nutrition and health. The programme will include the co-ordination of medical and epidemiological research, raising public awareness, and promoting pilot projects which improve nutritional status. Attention will also be given to the problems associated with alcohol abuse. Much of this activity may take place under the umbrella of a 'European Year of Nutrition' and 1994 has been designated for this purpose.[11]

Public Health Campaigns

Under the objective of raising the standard of living, the EC has been able to fund a number of public health campaigns. In 1987 a 'Europe Against Cancer' programme was launched, committing the EC to action on several fronts, including campaigns to reduce smoking and to improve national diets.[12] The stated aim of the programme is to reduce mortality from cancer in Europe by 15% by the year 2000. Information exchange on health education and medical research on AIDs in the EC have received a budget of 5.5 million ECUs (approximately £3.85 million). A campaign to combat drug-abuse has been launched, and it seems likely that there will be a campaign on the prevention of heart disease in the near future.

Pharmaceuticals

An important effect of 1992 in those European countries that have relatively high standards of drug safety, including the UK, could be a deterioration in standards of control of pharmaceuticals.[13] Medicines have been treated as a consumer good within the SEA, whereas health-care services have not, and thus fall within the scope of harmonisation. This means that by the beginning of 1993 or soon afterwards there will be a common system of drug regulation in Europe. Hodgkin[14] has argued that this is almost certain to result in a levelling down rather than a levelling up of drug safety standards throughout the EC.

THE ROLE OF THE VOLUNTARY AND COMMUNITY SECTORS

To date, the major involvement of UK voluntary organisations concerned with health in European issues has been through the activities of the WHO Europe. In particular, the WHO 'Health for All Strategy'[15] and European Charter on Environment and Health[16] have been important points of reference for the public health movement in the UK, and several UK voluntary and community organisations are involved in the WHO 'Healthy Cities' network.[17] It is only recently that the voluntary and community sectors have begun to focus on 1992 and the role of the EC in health issues. Some organisations have reported that one of the future challenges will be to encourage greater collaboration between the European Commission and WHO Europe.

Health-oriented groups are recognising that the advent of the single market and the possibility of further moves towards economic and political union within the EC mean that policy formulation in Brussels and Strasbourg plays a significant part in influencing policies that affect health in member states. The Coronary Prevention Group, for example, claim that in terms of their campaigning work, they were partly 'driven to Brussels' by the realisation that policies concerned with, for example tobacco or food labelling, increasingly are being decided in Brussels rather than at a national level.

Some voluntary organisations have identified the significance of the CAP for health. Organisations such as the Coronary Prevention Group, the National Forum for CHD Prevention, and Consumers in the European Community Group have pointed out that while the EC has given some attention to nutritional issues through the *consumer-oriented* initiatives described above, health considerations are almost entirely absent from the instrument controlling the *production* of food in the EC - the CAP. The EC has a chronic over-production precisely in those areas where nutritionalists advise a reduction in consumption levels - butter, sugar and beef. These organisations, and others such as the European Bureau for Action on Smoking Prevention (BASP), are also highlighting the fact that through the CAP the EC subsidises the tobacco growing industry by nearly £800 million a year. The British government alone spends about £47 million annually through the EC on tobacco subsidies, in contrast to approximately £1 million on smoking education through the EC 'Europe Against Cancer' campaign. The British and Belgian governments are currently the only countries supporting a reduction of CAP subsidies for tobacco production.[18]

In the last few years the Coronary Prevention Group, along with the equivalent groups in Denmark and the Netherlands, has played a pioneering role in the development of the International Heart Network[19] (IHN), a network of non-profit, non-government organisations campaigning to raise the issue of heart disease prevention at EC level. The IHN employs a lobbyist based in Brussels, and has provided briefings (for example, on EC proposals to limit the tar yield of tobacco, improve health warning labels on tobacco products, and introduce standardised nutrition labelling) for members of the Economic and Social Committee (Appendix C) and for MEPs on the Parliamentary Committee on Environment, Public Health and Consumer Protection. IHN has also campaigned for EC tax policies to recognise the need for governments to continue to use the price of tobacco products as an instrument of health policy.

The lack of EC competence in the health field means that organisations such as IHN describe their campaigning work as having to be 'through the back door', by which they mean their arguments have to be linked to trade rather than to health issues. The challenge, according to Health Action International (an organisation concerned with the safety of pharmaceuticals)[20] is for groups to be 'developing ideas about what a European health policy should contain and arguing for that, instead of permitting important health issues to be tacked on to discussions about trade and tariff barriers'.[21]

Another challenge for health pressure groups is to counter the work of lobbyists from the tobacco, food and drink, and pharmaceutical industries at a European level. IHN suggest that the influence of the tobacco lobby:

may have contributed to the fact that proposals on restricting smoking in public places have been downgraded from the status of a directive (which would have the force of law) to a mixed resolution (which does not). The influence of sectors of the food industry is also apparent. An international confectionery firm was known to have influence on an EC committee considering the nutrition labelling proposals. The committee's opinion was weakened as a result.[22]

Thus, Hodgkin argues:

health professionals, consumer groups and other public interest groups will have to learn the rules of the European game and will have to put human and financial resources into this area. If they do not, the field will be left open for industry lobbyists and the long term penalties for consumers and for health will be costly.[23]

There are a number of further signs of increasing involvement of the UK voluntary and community sectors in EC issues. In September 1990 the Public Health Alliance (PHA) organised a national conference on '1992: The People's Health', which aimed to act as a springboard for action on public health in Europe. The PHA has successfully bid for funding (with ECAS) from WHO Europe to explore further the role of non-government organisations in European health policy, and a European PHA is in the initial stages of development.[24] The National Community Health Resource published an edition of its newsletter featuring Europe, which explores the implications of the new Europe and the opportunities and threats it presents to community groups and local health initiatives.[25] UK cancer organisations have been active in the 'Europe Against Cancer' programme, and alcohol agencies are beginning to monitor the implications of EC policy for their area of work.[26]

Increasingly, ECAS provides a focus for campaigning work and information on EC and health issues. ECAS believes that health is an area set to develop in terms of the EC's areas of competence. It argues that there is an urgent need for the Commission to address the contradiction between the lack of a European legal basis for health on the one hand, and the enormous expansion of the EC impact on health policies and standards on the other. One of ECAS's priorities is to campaign for health policy to be addressed in the forthcoming revision of the treaties. The six points ECAS have identified as a first basis for discussion about future EC work in the health sector are reproduced in Box M.

FUTURE EC WORK IN THE HEALTH SECTOR: THE VIEW OF ECAS

1   The European Parliament should consider whether to include public health in the current discussion for revision of the Treaty. Public health needs a firmer basis, like environment and social affairs, in the Treaty.

2   In areas such as health, the principle of subsidiarity cannot be misused to conclude that the whole sector is either in the national or in the EC framework. It is obvious that most activity currently in train - health standards for products, co-ordination of research - automatically has a European dimension, whilst many other aspects of the health care system reflecting different traditions and priorities will remain in the national preserve. The European Parliament should investigate the scope and limits of an EC health policy, which currently does not exist.

3   There should be some mechanism such as a Senior Commissioner responsible for co-ordinating the health-related activities among different Commission departments (DG I, III, V, VI, VIII, XI, XII, XIII). The development of separate agencies for the evaluation of medicines, for the environment and possibly for food and health, hygiene and safety, raise the issue of co-ordination. Many might argue for a single Agency, but this would not allow for the necessary specialisation.

4   A common database on health issues should be set up covering medical research, assessment of substances which might damage health, and the monitoring of instances of disease, handicap, accidents and adverse drug reactions, food poisoning, etc. The data should be publicly accessible and shared among the various agencies under discussion.

5   There are over 80 consultative committees in the health area and there may be a need to rationalise their activities. A consultative committee on health was once suggested. In any case, there is an evident need to involve voluntary sector non-profit associations which are playing an increasingly important role in relation to health ministries and services.

6   Health ministers should meet as a Council at least once every six months as a real decision-making body, like their colleagues for the environment.

Source: *The European Citizen*, 1991 Euro-Citizen-Action-Service.

CONCLUSION

The 1980s saw a re-emergence of a strong public health movement in the UK, in which voluntary and community organisations have played a crucial role. The year 1992 has given this movement a new European focus, as increasingly many of the decisions affecting the public health are being decided in Brussels rather than at a national level. The EC is now clearly established as an important focus for occupational health legislation. Some organisations are optimistic that the EC will expand its role in the area of public health and will place EC health policy on a firmer legal footing. Others believe that this scenario is wishful thinking on the part of pressure groups, and believe that such developments are extremely unlikely in either the short or the long-term. Whichever direction developments take, it will be important that voluntary and community organisations concerned with improvements in the public health are active participants in European debates.

REFERENCES

1   Gough, I. and Baldwin-Edwards, M. (1990) 'The Impact of EC Membership on Social Security and Health in the UK' in Mangeen, S., Hantrais, L., and O'Brien, M. (eds) *The Implications of 1992 for Social Insurance.* Cross-national Research Group, University of Aston, Birmingham.

2   McCarthy, M. (1991) 'Health care in the European Community - the significance of the single market', *Critical Public Health*, 1991, 1, pp6-10.

3   Research by Fox and Adelstein quoted in Public Health Alliance (1990) *1992: The People's Health: Who's in Charge?* Report of a one day conference held to explore the relationship between public health and Europe in September 1990. Available from PHA, Room 204, Snow Hill House, 10-15 Livery Street, Birmingham, B3 2NU.

4   USDAW (1990) *Europe 1992: The USDAW Workbook.* USDAW, 188 Wilmslow Road, Manchester, M14 6LJ.

5   Quoted in Labour Research Department (1990) *Worker's Rights and 1992: the LRD Guide to the Social Charter and Action Programme.* LRD Publications, 78 Blackfriars Road, London SE1 8HF.

6   For further details on the health and safety directives see Labour Research Department, *Worker's Rights and 1992*.

7   The information in this section is taken from Sharp, I. and Young, A. (1991) *Tobacco policy - the impact of the European Community and 1992*. Briefing paper for the National Forum for Coronary Heart Disease Prevention and the Health Education Authority.

8   Action on Smoking and Health (1991) *Brief on the Proposed European Directive to Ban All Tobacco Advertising*, ASH, London.

9   For further details see Sharp and Young, *Tobacco policy*.

10   Longfield, J. (1991) *Annual Report 1990 of the International Heart Network's European Community Office*. Available from the Coronary Prevention Group, 102 Gloucester Place, London, W1H 3DA.

11   Longfield, *Annual Report 1990 of the International Heart Network*.

12   CEC (1989a) *Europe against Cancer* CE-54-88-013-EN-C Luxembourg; CEC (1989b) *Europe Against Cancer Programme: Outline for an Action Plan 1990-1994*. SEC(89) 648 Brussels.

13   The information in this section is taken from Hodgkin, C. (1991) '1992 - Is Harmonisation Healthy?' *Critical Public Health*, 1991, 1, pp11-17.

14   Hodgkin, '1992 - Is Harmonisation Healthy?'

15   WHO (1981), *Global Strategy for 'Health for All by the Year 2000'*, WHO, Geneva.

16   WHO Europe (1990), *European Charter on Environment and Health*, WHO, Copenhagen, Denmark.

17   The UK 'Health for All' Network can be contacted at PO Box 101, Liverpool L69 FBE. The address for the EURONET European Network of the WHO Healthy Cities Project is Healthy Cities Office, WHO (Copenhagen), 8, Scherfigsvej, DK-2100, Copenhagen.

18   Sharp and Young, *Tobacco Policy*.

19   Further details on the International Heart Network can be obtained from the Coronary Prevention Group (address above).

20   Health Action International are based at Jacob van Lennepkade 334 T, 1053 NJ Amsterdam.

21   Hodgkin, '1992 - Is Harmonisation Healthy?'

22   Longfield, *Annual Report 1990 of the International Heart Network*.

23   Hodgkin, '1992 - Is Harmonisation Healthy?'

24   For further details, contact the Public Health Alliance (address above).

25   National Community Health Resource (1990) '1992: How Will it Affect Local Communities?' *Community Health Action*, November.

26   For further details contact GLAAS (Greater London Association of Alcohol Services).

8

The Environment

INTRODUCTION

World concern for the protection of the environment began to develop in the early 1970s. A United Nations conference on the environment in Stockholm in 1972 made a call for concerted action. During the 1970s and 1980s disasters such as Chernobyl illustrated the threats to the environment, while scientific evidence highlighted the effects of acid rain and possible damage to the ozone layer from the use of CFCs, and the destruction of the tropical rain forests. In addition, there were calls for greater use of renewable forms of energy.

When the Treaty of Rome was signed in 1957 there was no provision for taking action on environmental matters. The aim was to have sustained rather than sustainable growth. Some of the environmental concerns outlined above were discussed at the 1972 European Council (comprising the heads of state, Appendix C) in Paris. It was agreed at this meeting that the goal of economic expansion should not be an end in itself, and that special attention should be paid by the EC to the protection of the environment.[1] The meeting thus laid the ground for Community action on the environment. The first Community action programme on the environment covered the years 1973-1977 and there have been three further programmes since then. A considerable amount has been achieved since 1973, including legislation on the quality of drinking and bathing water, the control of air pollution from industrial sources, limits on car and aircraft noise levels, controls over new small car emissions, and the protection of wild birds. Indeed, over 100 environmental EC directives have already been passed. However, it is interesting to note that the proper legal basis for action was only established with the passing of the SEA in 1986.

This chapter begins by illustrating some of the ways in which the single European market could have a deleterious effect on Europe's environment. It then looks at some of the key initiatives taken by the EC in the

126

environmental field, and describes the campaigning agendas of the voluntary environmental movement in Europe.

THE EFFECTS OF THE SINGLE EUROPEAN MARKET

The single market is an economic programme which aims to achieve higher levels of growth in the economies of the EC member states. There is always the danger, however, that economic growth will be harmful to the environment if there are no accompanying controls on the form of that growth.[2] For example, one of the aims of the single market is to eliminate barriers to the transportation of goods between member states. This will result in an increased amount of road freight, particularly in view of the opening up of Eastern Europe to trade with the Community. One commentator estimates that the amount of road freight in Europe will approximately double,[3] resulting in higher fuel consumption, greater air pollution and increased pressure for road building.

The Cecchini Report[4] estimated that the single European market should lead to an increase in the GDP of member states and the disposable incomes of Europeans. If this happens, there could be, for example, more retail and housing developments, and consequently an increase in areas of built-upon land. As GDP rises, tourism also increases and so does the infrastructure associated with tourism, such as airports, hotels and car parks. Tourism can harm the very things in the natural environment that tourists come to see. And, an increase in disposable incomes means more consumption, which brings additional problems of waste-disposal.[5]

There are particular concerns about the less-developed economies of the southern European countries. Encouraging economic development in these countries may harm undisturbed habitats and local environments. Clearly these countries cannot, and should not, be denied the advantages of development that the northern European countries already have. But it may be possible to learn from the experience of these countries and to introduce safeguards that will reduce the harmful effects of development.

Concerns about the effect of growth on Europe's environment have been backed up by an increasing awareness that pollution does not respect national boundaries. One example of this in Europe is the highly polluted Rhine river which flows through a number of countries. Pollution entering the river at one point has an effect at all points downstream and in many different countries. Similarly, emissions into the North Sea at any point can affect the coastlines of several countries, and emissions which cause acid rain can be discharged by one country, and the effects felt in many countries.

EC INITIATIVES

The SEA reflects the Community's decision to take a more definite position on the environment. Article 130 of the Act specifically refers to the environment, and states that action by the Community relating to the environment shall have the following three objectives:

- to preserve, protect and improve the quality of the environment;

- to contribute towards protecting human health;

- to ensure a prudent and rational utilisation of natural resources.

Article 130 includes the principles of preventive action, rectification of pollution at source, and the polluter paying. It also stipulates that environmental protection requirements shall be a component of the Community's other policies. Action should only be taken at the level of the Community when the objectives of the policy can be better attained at that level rather than at member state level, following the principle of subsidiarity (page 26). In the main, the financing of any necessary measures is the responsibility of member states. Importantly, Article 130 states that decisions about environmental matters have to be taken unanimously, except where there is unanimous agreement that decisions can be taken by majority voting.

Although the SEA was passed in 1986, it was not until late 1988 that the Council of Ministers commissioned a task force to examine the environmental consequences of 1992. The conclusion of the task force, when it reported in November 1989, was that the single market was potentially environmentally unsustainable. The report concluded that 'the importance of the single market is that by accelerating economic growth, it renders more acute issues which arise from the growth process.'[6] One particularly striking example from the task force's report is that, despite the implementation of environmental policies to cut emissions of sulphur dioxide and nitrogen oxide, which result in acid rain, from power stations and cars, these will still increase by 8-9 per cent and 12-14 per cent respectively by 2010.[7]

The Community took further action at the meeting of the Council of Ministers in Dublin in June 1990 when a 'Declaration on the Environment' was adopted.[8] The meeting agreed that 'a more enlightened and more systematic approach to environmental management is urgently needed'.[9] The Declaration stated that action 'will be developed on a co-ordinated basis and on the principles of sustainable development and preventative and precautionary action'. It highlighted issues such as the depletion of the ozone layer, man-made emissions of greenhouse gases, and the destruction of the tropical rain forests. It also recognised the special problems of the developing world and Central and Eastern Europe. The Commission was urged to continue the monitoring of environmental issues in the Community and to prepare a fifth action programme for the environment, a draft of which is to be presented in 1991.

The action programme currently in force is the fourth one. Priority areas include:

- the reduction at source of pollution and nuisance in various areas of industry;

- the control of chemical substances and preparations;

- the prevention of industrial accidents;

- measures on the evaluation and best use of biotechnology with regard to the environment;

- the protection of Europe's natural heritage;

- the encouragement of agricultural practices which are environmentally beneficial.

Four other policy initiatives are worth noting. Firstly, in 1985 the Community adopted a directive on environmental impact assessment which came into effect in 1988. This requires an environmental impact assessment to be considered as part of the planning approval process for a range of major industrial, infrastructure and agricultural projects. It is likely that the Commission will be prosecuting the British government for failing to undertake such assessments on certain road proposals.[10]

Secondly, a Green Paper has been produced on the urban environment.[11] This suggests a number of lines of action on urban planning, including financial assistance to pilot projects aimed at revitalising less favoured urban areas; urban transport (including encouraging innovative approaches to public transport); enhancing the historical heritage of European cities; urban industry; urban energy management and urban waste. Most of these initiatives are either research, funding of pilot projects or encouraging the exchange of good practice. While local authorities and other bodies concerned with the urban environment in the UK have generally welcomed the Green Paper, there have been concerns about the appropriate role of the Commission in this area, and a desire to ensure that action primarily remains with local authorities and local agencies, according to the principle of subsidiarity (page 26).

Thirdly, there has been agreement to establish a European Environmental Agency. The Agency will collect and assess data on the environment so that it can monitor the application of Community legislation. However, it has not been given any powers of regulation.

Fourthly, a proposal by the Commission for a European eco-label has met with general approval by the Council of Ministers. The eco-label scheme would be a voluntary scheme to identify products that meet agreed EC environmental criteria. It would aim to give guidance to consumers, while encouraging waste minimisation, pollution reduction, and responsible use of non-renewable resources.

The major EC funding programme in the area of the environment is the Programme of Regional Action on the Initiative of the Commission concerning the Environment (ENVIREG)[12]. This is aimed at helping the poorest countries to preserve their environment while creating the foundation for balanced economic development. There are four specific objectives:

- to reduce the pollution of coastal areas, particularly in the Mediterranean regions;

- to promote the planning of land use in coastal areas in such a way as to preserve natural beauty and enhance biotopes;

- to contribute to the better control and management of toxic and hazardous industrial waste;

- to strengthen know-how relating to the design and management of facilities for reducing pollution and, more generally, to improve the ways in which environmental problems are tackled.

There is a budget of 500 million ECUs (approximately £350 million) from the Structural Funds for ENVIREG, and grants can be given both for construction works for suitable infrastructure and for research and feasibility studies. The primary aim will be to construct models of good practice.

THE ROLE OF THE VOLUNTARY AND COMMUNITY SECTORS

The European environmental lobby is not generally in favour of the single market as presently constituted, as it is likely to result in more harm to the environment. The European network for national environmental organisations is the European Environmental Bureau (EEB), based in Brussels.[13] Twenty-three UK organisations are members of the Bureau, including the Civic Trust, Friends of the Earth, Green Alliance, the Council for the Protection of Rural England, and the Royal Society for the Protection of Birds. Member organisations tend to fall into two groups: those interested in the protection of nature (strongly represented by UK organisations) and those interested in the reduction of pollution.

The EEB would like to see a number of fundamental changes to EC policy and action on the environment, including:

- The Community agreeing to contribute financially to global funds for the protection of the environment.

- The amendment of the General Agreement on Tariffs and Trade (GATT) rules to provide the means to control any trade dangerous to the environment.

- A revision to the treaties to allow a formal recognition of five major principles:

  - that the objective of Community action is to guarantee citizens the right to a clean and healthy environment;

  - that the Community should have competence in all sectors concerned with environmental protection;

  - that there should be differential integration, with the Community setting minimum standards;

  - that the internal market should be sustainable and environmentally sound;

  - that there should be free access to information on the environment.

- Improvements to structures and procedures, including the following recommendations:

  - that the co-operation procedure and voting by qualified majority (Chapter 1) should extend to all environmental matters;

  - that compliance with Community directives should be an incontestable rule;

  - that there should be an EC Inspectorate for the environment;

- that citizens and non-governmental organisations should be allowed to go the European Court of Justice, which should have the right to financially sanction member states for infringements;

- that there should be an EC integrated-action programme and the establishment of an environment fund.

The EEB produces a memorandum every six months for the incoming president of the Community. This memorandum highlights areas of progress and areas of concern and identifies priorities for the next six months. The memorandum produced in July 1990[14] considered that progress had been made in the previous year in that a Declaration on the Environment has been adopted (page 128), reports on energy, waste, urban environment and agriculture have been published, directives on waste and free access to environmental information have been adopted, and limit values for dangerous substances discharged into water have been fixed. However, the EEB memorandum listed the following areas as failures:

- the incapacity of the Commission to adopt a credible urgency plan to counterbalance the adverse effects of the single market;

- the lack of compliance with directives by member states and the refusal of member states to agree to an EC Inspectorate;

- lack of progress on the monitoring of water quality;

- the likely impact on the environment of projects funded under the Structural Funds without quality environmental impact assessments;

- the failure to agree a proposal on free access to information;

- the failure to present a strategy for the protection of tropical rain forests.

CONCLUSION

Despite a lot of discussion within the Community and considerable action, environmental issues are still peripheral to EC policy. Only about 0.1 per cent of the Community budget is spent on the environment. The basic aim of the single market is to achieve economic growth. Even the use of the Community's own funds, mainly the Structural Funds, are not tied closely into environmental considerations. The need to achieve unanimity among the member states and the limitations of the EC co-operation procedure (page

23) mean that decisions about environmental matters can be easily blocked by individual states. Those directives that are agreed have not been well implemented within the individual states. For example, the Commission has had to open proceedings against the British government in the Court of Justice over its tardiness in implementing measures to improve water quality. The aim of European voluntary organisations will be to change this state of affairs by arguing for reform of the treaties to give environmental affairs a stronger legal base, while continuing to lobby on a wide range of particular concerns.

REFERENCES

1   Lodge, J. (ed) (1989) *The European Community and the Challenge of the Future*. Pinter.

2   Robins, N. (1991) *A European Environmental Charter*. Fabian Pamphlet 543.

3   Personal communication from the European Environmental Bureau.

4   Cecchini, *The European Challenge*.

5   Haigh, N. and Baldock, D. (1989) *Environmental Policy and 1992*. Report prepared for Department of the Environment by the Institute for European Environmental Policy.

6   Quoted in Robins, *A European Environmental Charter*.

7   From Robins, *A European Environmental Charter*.

8   European Council (1990) *Declaration on the Environment - The Environmental Imperative*.

9   European Council, *Declaration on the Environment*.

10   *The Guardian*, June 1991.

11   CEC (1990) *Green Paper on the Urban Environment*, CEC, Brussels.

12   CEC (1990) *ENVIREG The Environment: a key to the development of least-favoured regions*, EC C115/03

13   The European Environmental Bureau can be contacted at Maison Européen de l'Environnement, rue de Luxembourg 20, B-1040 Brussels.

14   European Environmental Bureau (1990) *Memorandum to the Italian Presidency*, available from the EEB (address above).

9

Consumers

INTRODUCTION

Nearly everything that the Community does is likely to have an effect on consumers. It cannot be assumed that consumer concerns are limited to issues such as product safety and prices. They are as broad-ranging as the effects of monetary union on consumers, and of competition policy on air fares. This chapter looks at the likely effects of the single European market on consumers and at EC initiatives in the area of consumer policy. It then explores the role that voluntary and community organisations have played in making sure that consumer interests are represented at EC level.

THE EFFECTS OF THE SINGLE EUROPEAN MARKET

The Cecchini Report predicted that the creation of the single market should bring an increase in the range of choices available to consumers, as well as substantial savings due to lower production costs and wider competition:

> Put simply, consumers will be better off. Be they private individuals or intermediary businesses, the outlook is unreservedly good... European consumers will be paying a similar price for the same item. And, as the item will tend to be produced in the cheapest way, the level of this price will be on a downward journey.[1]

However, the effects of the single European market, and of EC policy generally, are likely to be more disparate and divisive than Cecchini suggests. To give some examples:

- The Commission's wish to bring VAT rates and excise duties into line across Europe (page 34) could increase prices in the UK on goods such as food, fuel, fares, publications, children's clothing and shoes, which all currently have a zero-rating for VAT. This would particularly affect those consumers who are less well-off. On the other hand, economic and monetary union would be likely to bring more stability for those consumers undertaking long-term financial commitments in other countries.

- The results of the 1991 round of discussions held under the General Agreement on Tariffs and Trade (GATT), and the general development of EC trade policy, will have important implications for the range of goods available to consumers and the prices of such goods. It cannot be assumed that the range of products available in the EC will increase. For example, the quota system which limits EC imports of cheaper clothing and shoes from developing countries as part of a protectionist policy against non-EC products could mean less rather than more choice for the consumer.

- Increased trade in foodstuffs and drink after 1992 will make it all the more important that food is labelled and defined in a standard way that is understood in all countries.

- Standards of control of pharmaceutical products in the UK post-1992 could deteriorate (page 119), and could mean that consumers are exposed to increased health risks in terms of drug safety as a result of the single European market.

Other areas which may be affected by increasing European integration and a single European market include the price of air travel, as 1992 is likely to provide an additional impetus to deregulation of the airfares market, and controls on direct mailing (Chapter 2, page 40).

EC INITIATIVES

The Community has always recognised the needs of consumers. A committee of trades union and consumer organisation representatives was set up as early as 1962, but proper consultation began in 1972 when the heads of state summit in Paris gave the go-ahead to a consumer policy, arguing that economic development must be translated into improved quality of life. The decision had three practical results:

- A consumer policy service was set up in the Commission.

- A Consumers Consultative Committee was created, with representatives of European consumer organisations.

- A first programme for consumer protection and information was adopted. This programme emphasised five fundamental rights: the right to health and safety, the right to redress, the right to the protection of economic interests, the right to representation and the right to information and education.

The initial work by the Commission was to attempt to harmonise all the different standards concerned with a particular consumer product. However, the Commission has been 'overtaken time and again: a hundred new standards are created at national level in the time it takes to harmonise a single one at European level'.[2] Following a judgement of the European Court of Justice in 1979, which decided that any product which has been legally manufactured and marketed in one member state must generally be admitted to the market of another member state, the Community developed a new approach to regulation problems based upon the principle of mutual recognition of the national rules in force. So Community directives need only define the essential health and safety requirements to be met by products. National products which meet these requirements can then be sold in any Community country.

By 1985, the Council of Ministers considered it necessary to adopt a 'New Impetus for Consumer Protection Policy', as it was felt that action to date had not been suffficient. This listed a number of areas for action, including nutrition labelling, cosmetics labelling, guarantees and after-sales service, package holidays, inflammibility of clothing and furniture, unfair contract terms and advertising, and access to justice. The single European market was seen as having a beneficial effect on prices. However, it was also accepted that the market by itself could not be relied upon to provide benefits to the consumer. In 1989, therefore, the Council of Ministers and the European Parliament agreed to a new three-year plan for 1990-1992.

The new plan identifies four priority concerns:

- **Ensuring that the voice of the consumers is better heard.** To this end the role of the Consumers' Consultative Council is to be developed, consumer organisations are to be promoted, especially in the least prosperous regions, and dialogue and co-operation between producers and consumers is to be encouraged.

136

- **Improving communication to consumers**. This will be through pilot local initiatives and policies that encourage awareness of what is involved when buying something, including comparisons between different products.

- **Better guarantees for consumers safety**, for example, by modifying legislation with respect to cosmetics, and establishing a list of products requiring special attention by consumers.

- **Improving the ability of consumers to undertake transactions throughout the Community**, for example, by simplifying and harmonising cross-border contracts, guarantees and after-sales service, and by improving consumers' access to justice and to compensation for damages.

THE ROLE OF THE VOLUNTARY AND COMMUNITY SECTORS

Consumers in the UK have been well organised for some time. Indeed the UK consumer movement is probably the biggest and the best organised in the Community. In general, the consumer movement is better organised in the northern countries of the Community, with Belgium, the Netherlands, Germany, and France the strongest after the UK. Denmark and Luxemburg have well established consumer organisations while Ireland, Portugal, Italy and Spain are relatively weak. Greece has little at the present time. The northern European countries are assisting the southern countries to develop their consumer movements.[3]

One reason for the long-standing involvement of UK consumer organisations in EC issues is that the British government has from an early date consulted them on draft proposals from the Commission. In order to make their voice more effective, organisations such as the Consumers' Association, the National Consumer Council and the National Federation of Women's Institutes came together to form the Consumers in the European Community Group (CECG). CEGG tend to take a pragmatic view of proposals coming from the Commission, in that EC proposals which might not otherwise be on the agenda in the UK and will clearly benefit consumers, will be supported. Where it is considered that proposals will be damaging to consumers, they are resisted.[4] To date, UK policies on consumer rights have been relatively advanced compared with other member states, so many of the proposals from the EC may not add a great deal to the rights of consumers in the UK.

The European network for consumer organisations is the European Bureau of Consumer Unions (BEUC). This has been in existence for over 20 years and has 17 full members from EC countries. BEUC campaigns, lobbies and provides information on consumer issues within the Community. Its work is largely determined by the proposals coming from the Commission, and at any one time BEUC will be deciding its position on up to 60 different proposals. Given the strength of the UK consumer movement, UK organisations play a prominent part in the workings of BEUC.

BEUC had representatives on the Consumers Consultative Committee, which, until recently, was the name of the formal mechanism whereby the Commission consulted with the consumer movement. The 33 members of the Committee's Council were nominated by BEUC, COFACE (the network for family organisations), ETUC (the trades unions) and EUROCOOP (representing consumer co-operatives). There were also experts appointed by the Commission. The role and effectiveness of the Committee was widely criticised.[5] It was felt that its views were often not taken into account by the Commission, and that it was consulted after decisions had already been made. It was also felt that the Committee was not truly representative of consumers. As a result of these concerns, the Committee was reorganised in 1990 and renamed the Consumers Consultative Council. Each of the four organisations mentioned above still have the right to nominate four members of the Council but they will now be joined by 17 representatives of national consumer organisations and six independent experts chosen by the Commission (39 members in total). However, consumer groups are still concerned that the secretariat is not independent of the Commission and that the Council still includes trades union representatives, whom it is felt may have interests contrary to those of consumers. There were also pressures from some member states to have producers represented on the Council but this was opposed by the consumer organisations and has not been agreed.

The CAP is one key area of concern to European consumers. A major conflict exists between the aims of the CAP and the needs of consumers. It has been estimated that the policy now costs a family of four in the EC on average £16 per week on food bills and in tax.[6] The problem is that the CAP guarantees a market to farmers for whatever they produce, at guaranteed minimum prices which misjudge the level of surpluses, supply, demand and world prices. According to CEGG:

> we are paying five times over for the Common Agricultural Policy. We pay higher prices for food. We pay for the surplus food to be bought from the farmer. We pay for its storage in intervention. We pay for the massive subsidies needed to sell it at a loss to non-EEC countries, and for destruction of unsaleable surplus food.[7]

138

The solution advocated by consumer groups is to cut support prices to curb over-production, and if necessary to switch to direct income support for farmers, and to provide incentives for farmers to develop other ways of generating an income from the countryside, for example, alternative farm products and new market niches such as organic produce, venison, and angora, farm holidays for tourists, and conservation projects.

Finally, consumer groups are concerned about the relatively small resources that the Commission devotes to consumer protection and information, and about the meagre level of resources which the consumer movement has to lobby the Commission and argue its case, compared with the powerful producer lobbies. While the EC spends 975 million ECUs (approximately £682.5 million) on subsidising tobacco production in the EC, the total of the consumer protection and information budget in 1989 was only three million ECUs (just over £2 million).

CONCLUSION

In general, the consumer movement welcomes the moves towards a single market in Europe. It is felt that deregulation will benefit consumers by allowing greater choice and an ability to shop around to achieve the lowest price. The concerns are that the process will not go fast enough as the interests of employers and national interests are used to maintain protection in certain areas. The consumer movement will be watching developments carefully, to see that there is real benefit to the consumer, and in particular, that the interests of the producers do not dominate. It will be arguing for a much higher profile for consumer issues in EC policy, and for a greater role for the consumer movement in European Community affairs.

REFERENCES

1   Cecchini, *The European Challenge*.

2   CEC (1990) *The European Community and Consumer Protection*, European File 14/90.

3   Interview with European Bureau of Consumer Unions, February 1991.

4   Interview with Consumers in the European Community Group, January 1991.

5   CECG (1989) *Participation of Consumers in National and European Community Policy Making in the Run Up to 1992 and Thereafter.* Submission to Committee on the Environment, Public Health, and Consumer Protection of the European Parliament.

6   Consumers in the European Community Group (1991), *Annual Report 1990.* Available from CECG, 24 Tufton Street, London SW1 3RB.

7   CECG (Consumers in the European Community Group) (1987) *Could Do Better Towards An EEC Policy for Consumers.* Available from CECG.

PART THREE

10

Summing Up the Issues

INTRODUCTION

What are the implications of the far-reaching European changes described in the previous chapters of this report for the future policies and work of voluntary and community organisations? How can organisations best prepare to meet the challenges and opportunities presented by the rapidly emerging European community? In this concluding chapter, the range of impacts discussed in this report are summarised under four broad headings:

- Changes in the socio-economic context.

- The development of new principles and frameworks for social policy.

- Changes in policy-making processes and structures.

- Legislative, financial and fiscal changes.

Within this framework, the views and evidence collected and developed by the research team are used to analyse how voluntary and community organisations can tackle the new challenges ahead.

THE RANGE OF IMPACTS

Changes in the Socio-Economic Context

The Cecchini Report predicts that the 1992 programme will 'provide the economic context for the regeneration of European industry in both goods and services... [and] will give a permanent boost to the prosperity of the people of Europe and indeed the world as a whole'.[1] According to this perspective, a substantial proportion of Europeans will enjoy improved social and economic conditions as a result of the single market. Chapter 9 described how consumer organisations generally support this view, believing that increased competition will lead to lower prices and a greater diversity of consumer products.

However, Cecchini also predicts that the single market could bring 'significant social and economic dislocations' to some population groups and certain communities. At least three major socio-economic changes have been identified in this report, all of which could dramatically alter the lives of individuals and communities during the 1990s.

First, Chapter 3 described how the creation of a more integrated and more competitive European market could set in motion a further wave of economic and industrial restructuring, which would have considerable impacts on many regions and local economies in terms of increased job loss and unemployment. Certain industries are particularly vulnerable (Table 2, Chapter 3, page 51), and the regions peripheral to the 'golden triangle' are likely to be most severely affected. Industrial restructuring will almost certainly lead to a greater concentration and centralisation of ownership and control over industry and employment in Europe. The drive towards a more flexible workforce to meet the needs of the leaner and more modernised European economy will also tend to create greater insecurity in the labour market, particularly for those who are already located in a marginal position, such as women and Black and ethnic minority workers.

Second, during the 1990s these economic changes will be accompanied by dramatic demographic changes in the population of Europe and exacerbated by a heavy increase in social needs. Specifically, the ageing of the European population is set to continue, and there will be less workers to support a growing number of pensioners. As discussed in Chapter 4, these changes have major implications, not only for the funding of welfare benefits and services, but also for the type of services that are needed. An additional dimension of demographic change is likely to be migration and immigration across the new map of Europe, although it is not yet clear what the effects of such movements will be.

Third, it is predicted that the combination of industrial dislocation and demographic changes described above will contribute to greater levels of social need and poverty in the Europe of the 1990s. Chapter 4 described the enormity of the problem facing those working to combat social deprivation in Europe: almost 15% of the European population are living on less than half the average incomes for their country, and will be too poor to become consumers in the single European market. The European Commission has

144

warned of 'social exclusion and marginalisation and the ... appearance of new forms of poverty' as a specific result of 1992.[2]

The emergence of such warnings about the possible adverse effects of a single European market has resulted in some voluntary and community organisations adopting an extremely cautious or critical view of 1992. Some have begun to ask whether the appropriate stance for the voluntary and community sectors should be one of opposition to the single market. A leading voluntary organisation posed the question: 'Why are we legitimising it by getting involved at all?'[3] However, many other organisations believe that the voluntary and community sectors, with their long history of solidarity with disadvantaged groups, must take up the challenge of championing the rights of socially marginalised groups at a European level, and more generally, of influencing the future shape of Europe.

The Development of New Principles and Frameworks for Social Policy

The participation of voluntary and community organisations in debates about the future of social policy in Europe will enable them 'to better *chose* the future we want, rather than trying to predict the future we might get'.[4] New frameworks and principles for social policy are emerging from the range of different welfare models that exist within Europe. The challenge will be to identify, develop and integrate the best from each model. Chapter 4 identified some of the opportunities for developing a more just welfare system by drawing upon concepts contained in the different models of welfare: the opportunities provided by the French concept of solidarity with the poor, and the innovative models of anti-poverty work highlighted by the Poverty 3 programme, for example. However, a melting-pot of welfare models carries dangers as well as opportunities, in that it allows policy-makers the possibility of selecting the cheapest solution for governments, rather than the best for social justice.

One dimension of the choices and changes currently facing European social policy is the question of whether social rights should be based on an individual's employment status, citizenship, or resident status in the European Community. There are concerns that the different European welfare states are converging towards a corporatist model, in which social rights are attached primarily to employment rather than to citizenship. This could reinforce the development of a dual-welfare system, where labour market arrangement takes care of those within the sphere of traditional employment through various corporate welfare schemes, but neglects or excludes marginal and less privileged groups in society. Commentators such as Townsend (page 71) see the Social Charter as encouraging these trends,

145

arguing that implementation of the Charter will exacerbate inequalities between those in work and those who are not in work. For non-European citizens, there are also dangers in social rights being linked to citizenship. Chapter 5 identified the criticism of Black and ethnic minority groups that at the same time as EC nationals receive greater freedoms and rights in the new Europe, migrant workers will be relegated to the status of second class citizens with minimal rights. More generally, there is a concern that protectionist economic policies are being replicated in the social field, and that 1992 will encourage a 'Fortress Europe' mentality, where the rights of Europeans are protected at the direct expense of non-Europeans, whose rights are neglected.

A second important dimension of the European social policy debate is whether moves towards convergence of welfare systems will result in a levelling up or a levelling down of standards thoughout Europe. There is a danger that the relatively advanced welfare systems of the northern European countries will be brought down to the standards of the others, rather than the poorer standards of the Mediterranean countries being brought up to the highest standards.

Other areas of concern to voluntary and community organisations which may be affected by trends towards European harmonisation or convergence have been identified in this report, such as the safety of pharmaceutical products and levels of VAT. An additional concern is being expressed by lesbian and gay groups, who are arguing that, given the current diversity between member states over basic rights concerning homosexuality, it is essential that there is a levelling up of laws to those of the most progressive states, such as Denmark and the Netherlands, rather than any levelling down.[5]

Some pressure groups have taken the opportunity to use European experiences and practice as arguments for raising levels of provision in the UK. For example, European countries have provided some groups with precedents which they have used to strengthen their arguments for change in the UK. Others have used a European 'league table' approach to highlight the UK's relatively poor position on a particular issue, and to argue for policy-change, for example, levels of childcare provision.

A third important European policy development is the principle of subsidiarity (page 26). This may help to counteract the centralising and privatising principles which have informed social policy in the UK for over a decade, and begin to provide a stronger constitutional basis for devolution and decentralisation of social policy to regional and local government levels.[6] It thus has important implications for voluntary and community organisations. The principle of subsidiarity links in with the current debate about where power would be located within a federal Europe. Palmer[7] argues that the essence of a federal constitution is that it would transfer power downwards to the regions and local communities, and believes that this is one reason why the British government is opposed to a federal future for Europe

146

- because it would be likely to give more power to the regions and take it away from the centre. Certainly, voluntary organisations in Scotland, Wales and Northern Ireland see Europe as offering opportunities to have a voice independent of their English counterparts.

Changes in Policy-Making Processes and Structures

Substantial changes are taking place in policy-making processes and structures in the UK and Europe, and these changes have major implications for the potential of voluntary and community organisations to influence policy developments at European, national and local levels.

First, there is a melting down of the traditional boundaries between the private, the public and the voluntary sectors - a far more mixed economy of welfare is emerging. This trend is likely to open up opportunties for an expanded role in welfare provision for the larger UK voluntary organisations that can win contracts, but could bring even more financial insecurity to smaller community organisations. In the longer term, the new roles and working relationships could bring tremendous challenges and opportunities to link agencies and ideas that have previously been quite separate. Abrahamson[8] has developed a useful model to illustrate the changing relationships between the private market, the state and civil society, which includes both the voluntary and the community sectors. He argues that the development of social policy in Europe will not be determined by a simple battle between market liberalism and state socialism, but by a more complex welfare pluralism, in which it is accepted that market, state and civil society will all play a role in welfare provision. In this welfare mix voluntary and community organisations will sometimes play the leading role, sometimes a subsidiary role and sometimes a complimentary role.

A second, and extremely significant change in the policy-making process is that the EC's method of working appears to be challenging the very concept of separate tiers of government, and instead is introducing a new model of interlocking spheres. The traditional picture of government as a vertical hierarchy with functions and responsibilities divided between separate rungs of a ladder is no longer adequate to explain the new European political process. Rather, it is becoming clear that in addition to their vertical relationships with the member states through national governments, the EC is actively cultivating horizontal relationships with regional and local authorities and with cross-national networks of organisations and interest-groups, including voluntary and community organisations.[9]

By developing a set of overlapping and interlocking spheres it may be possible to have a more plural and open form of policy-making than the centralised form of government that is more familiar to people in the UK. The implications of this for voluntary and community organisations is that if they are to have influence at a European level, organisations will need to develop cross-national links and perspectives, issue-based alliances, and skills in coalition-building. European networks therefore represent an important way in which voluntary and community sectors can contribute to changing the political process in Europe.

Legislative, Financial, and Fiscal Changes

Finally, this report has described some of the more practical implications of 1992 for voluntary and community organisations. Most obviously, to take advantage of the challenging new opportunities to help develop European social policy, voluntary and community organisations need adequate resources. Many organisations fear that lack of resources within the UK voluntary sector will preclude them from taking up the opportunities of new roles and spheres of influence in the 1990s. One community organisation commented: 'when you're struggling for survival, Europe is a bit of a luxury'. And, a CDF report has pointed out:

> All over Europe, governments and public authorities are seeking innovative ways to solve problems of disadvantaged localities and groups. The way forward is often seen as 'partnership' with local people. But there is little understanding that if partnership is to mean anything, it must involve building up the whole sector of independent local groups ..... just as a more positive dialogue is developing, the truly voluntary element in the voluntary sector is beginning to crumble before our eyes.[10]

A wide range of programmes of work that offer funding opportunities to organisations have been identified in this report. These are mostly small-scale in terms of the amount of money available for each programme, but still offer useful opportunities for funding to organisations in the UK. Larger-scale funding will continue to be available through the Structural Funds, although as explained in Chapter 3, the increase in the budget for these Funds is unlikely to benefit the UK very much, and there may well be a major re-orientation of their focus towards cross-national rather than national projects.

Chapter 2 outlined a number of specific legal and fiscal developments that will affect voluntary and community organisations. VAT approximation could affect zero-rating for charities, although in the short-term this danger seems to have receded, partly as a result of lobbying by voluntary bodies. The development of the contract culture in the UK will be reinforced by the EC rules on the opening up of public procurement to competition across frontiers.

148

Also mentioned were proposals on driver licences, protection of part-time and temporary workers, health and safety regulations, and the mutual recognition of professional qualifications. EC involvement in areas such as these is likely to increase in the future.

SHAPING THE FUTURE

Involvement in European activity has much to offer voluntary and community organisations. It offers incentives to learn languages, to travel and to develop new contacts and skills through increased experience of participation in international events. It will encourage the development of a European consciousness, both through exposure to the emerging policies and thinking of the EC, and through informal discussions with participants from other countries. It can provide opportunities to learn about different approaches and traditions of work, and to share examples of good practice. It can also enrich the quality and the texture of existing work both at national and local level. Above all, involvement in European activity offers exciting opportunities for organisations to influence the future of European social policy.

Until recently, many organisations have seen the EC primarily as a source of funding. However, this is changing rapidly, as more and more organisations see the wider potential for getting involved in European policy issues: 'Europe used to be looked upon as a pot of gold. Our whole attitude has changed. We've become more wide open as to what Europe can mean, rather than what it can give us. It's a place to open up horizons.'

The rapid moves towards integration of economic and social policies at European level has brought an upsurge of activity in campaigning and lobbying. A recent NCVO study on campaigning in the voluntary sector highlighted 'a mismatch between what organisations feel they should be doing and what they actually are doing', but noted that campaign activity in Europe is 'likely to increase significantly as aspirations are put effectively into practice'.[11]

What are the areas on which campaign activity is likely to be focused in the future? Those organisations working with the unemployed will be lobbying not just for grants for specific employment and training projects, but also for investment in local economic development, to create new jobs and to cushion some of the consequences of industrial restructuring. This report has identified many areas where the voluntary and community sectors will be wanting to lobby for an extension of the EC's competence. Those organisations working on environmental issues will want to argue for an extension of powers to control pollution and for a European enforcement agency. Other obvious examples are social housing (page 89), health (Chapter 7) and policies to tackle racism and discrimination (Chapter 5). Many voluntary and community organisations will be wanting to argue for a charter of citizens rights, with rights and obligations based upon citizenship rather than upon labour market participation, as in the present Social Charter. Women's organisations will want to ensure that Community legislations on equal rights is enforced and extended.

In addition to lobbying in Brussels and Strasbourg, one of the conclusions from this report is that voluntary organisations need to be aware of the importance of continuing to lobby at the national level. The anti-poverty lobby, for example, will want to see the ideas of the EC programmes to combat poverty extended into wider action, not only through increased Community funding, but also through more commitment to anti-poverty work from national governments. Organisations will continue to lobby for the British government to back the Social Charter, and to fight its opposition to draft directives that would improve the working conditions of part-time and temporary workers, and pregnant women.

The Power of European Networks

There is increasing recognition within the voluntary and community sectors that effective European lobbying requires a cross-national or even pan-European approach: 'Individual organisations from a single member state will carry comparatively little weight in the European policy context. Collaborative work which crosses national boundaries is essential'.[12]

The development of cross-national networks, some of which owe their existence to the Commission's role in promoting and financing them, is an important example of the different style of policy making processes and structures the EC is encouraging. They also represent an important way forward for the voluntary and community sectors to join and contribute to the political process in Europe. Organisations will want to gain expertise in operating in this environment, and will need to acquire new skills in cross-national communication.[13]

Keeping Informed about European Developments

The key to unlocking the 'Brussels box', as one organisation expressed it, is information. The voluntary and community sectors therefore need to ensure that they have a regular source of information on current developments. Sources of information about Europe are expanding all the time, and it is hard to keep pace with the stream of material. Many local authorities can help voluntary and community organisations with information about European policy developments, and developing this information source may have other positive implications for local partnerships. Appendix F describes how one local authority in Wales has identified the ways in which they can help voluntary and community groups. MEPs are another potential information source, although the European Parliament's relatively weak role in European policy making means that MEPs themselves find it difficult sometimes to keep abreast with Commission initiatives. Other useful information sources, including some regular bulletins on Europe produced specifically for voluntary and community organisations, are listed in Appendix E.

The Value of a Strategic Review

In the light of this report, voluntary and community organisations may wish to undertake a strategic review of their operations. Is the appointment of a European officer appropriate, or do all staff need to integrate a European dimension into their areas of work? Is a staff audit a useful way to assess the current level of knowledge of the EC which exists within the organisation - for example, the range of languages spoken and existing contacts in other member states? Does a European working group need to be established to further develop policy in this area? Are there any changes in needs or policies at a European level that will have an impact on the organisation or on the people it serves?

Support from National and European Umbrella Organisations and from Central Government

In taking European developments seriously and in developing a European dimension to their work, voluntary and community organisations do not need to re-invent the wheel every time. National bodies like the VSU, NCVO and CDF, and European bodies such as ECAS and ESAN, can help to circulate information and experience and to provide advice and training. A great deal can also be learned from other local voluntary and community organisations that have already gained some experience at the European level.

CONCLUSION

It is clear from our analysis that Europe is likely to be the arena for profound economic, political and social changes throughout the 1990s. This report has concentrated on the implications of the single market being created between 12 of the Western European countries. The upheavals in Eastern Europe are already stimulating a further wave of changes, with widespread repercussions for the European Community.

Although the sources of this restructuring are global or European, this report has shown that there are many direct and indirect consequences at the national and local levels. The key conclusion from our research is to reinforce the message 'think global, act local'. However, 'acting local' also increasingly involves linking up with similar organisations in other countries. The challenge therefore is for voluntary and community organisations to 'think global, act local', *and* network cross-nationally.

REFERENCES

1   Cecchini, *The European Challenge.*

2   Quoted in Robbins and Room, *Feasibility Study Report on Marginalisation.*

3   Quote from group interview with Scottish voluntary and community organisations, November, 1990.

4   Abrahamson, *Social Policy in Europe Towards Year 2000.*

5   See Association of Metropolitan Authorities (1991) *Equal Opportunity Implications of 1992: the Single European Market.* Report by Rashmi Patel. Available from AMA, 35 Great Smith Street, London SW1P 3BJ. For further information on the issues of concern to lesbian and gay groups and 1992, contact Stonewall, 2 Greycoat Place, Westminster, London, SW1P 1SB.

6   Spicker, P. *The Principle of Subsidiarity.*

7   Palmer, *The Federalists Are Not What They Seem.*

8   Abrahamson, P. (1991) *Social Policy in Europe Towards Year 2000: Social Integration or Social Differentiation?* Roskilde University, PO Box 260, DK-4000, Roskilde.

9   Schneider, V. (1989) *Policy Networks and the Decentralisation of Policy-Making*. EuroSocial Bulletin 55/56; Bryant, C. (1991) Europe and the European Community, 1992 Sociology 25:2 pp189-207.

10   Chanan, *Taken for Granted*.

11   NCVO (1990) *Cause and Effect: Campaigning and the Voluntary Sector*. NCVO.

12   NCVO, *Cause and Effect*.

13   For further information on European networks see Harvey, *Networking in Europe*.

APPENDICES

APPENDIX A

MEMBERS OF THE RESEARCH ADVISORY COMMITTEE

Gabriel Chanan	Community Development Foundation
Debbie Cooper	SKILL
Caroline Diehl	Community Service Volunteers Media Programme
Bronwen Fair	Voluntary Services Unit, Home Office
Don Flynn	Joint Council for the Welfare of Immigrants
Jane Goldsmith	National Alliance of Women's Organisations
Jeremy Harrison	European Consultant
Peter Kuenstler	CEI Consultants Ltd
Linda Lennard	National Consumer Council
Janet Lewis	Joseph Rowntree Foundation
Gordon Lishman	Age Concern England
Quintin Oliver	Northern Ireland Council for Voluntary Action
Chris Pond	Low Pay Unit
Bill Seary	European Social Action Network, Brussels (formerly NCVO)
Perri 6	National Council for Voluntary Organisations
Nigel Tarling	National Council for Voluntary Organisations
Marilyn Taylor	School of Advanced Urban Studies, University of Bristol
David Thomas	Community Development Foundation
Sylvie Tsyboula	Fondation de France, Paris

APPENDIX B

CANVASSING OPINION

One problem for a study like this was how to canvas opinions that reflected the diversity of roles, functions, and activities within the voluntary and community sectors (Chapter 3). A further problem was that many voluntary and community organisations were not sufficienty knowledgeable about European developments to form a view of their significance without some initial input. In devising a methodology for our investigation, we had to find a way of canvassing opinions from as broad a range of organisations as possible, and not just from those that were known to be involved in Europe. At the same time, the remit and time-scale of the study meant that we wanted to avoid contacting organisations with little or nothing to say about Europe.

In an attempt to address these problems, we developed a strategy that combined the following three methods of canvassing opinion. First, we conducted in-depth interviews with representatives from a range of voluntary organisations. Those selected for interview were chosen either because they had been identified by others as key actors in European activities, or because we saw them as representing a significant category of the voluntary sector in the context of this study. Second, we sent a semi-structured postal questionnaire to 100 organisations, all of which had previously registered for a day seminar on Europe organised by NCVO, CDF, and the European Briefing Unit. We were therefore selecting a sample of organisations that had shown some interest in Europe, and, through attendance at the seminars, had already been sensitised to some of the issues concerning the voluntary sector and Europe. Of the organisations surveyed, 30 per cent responded, a fair response rate for a postal questionnaire. Thirdly, we organised discussions about the social impact of 1992 for voluntary and community organisations at group events in Scotland and Wales. These events began with some initial input from the authors in order to stimulate further discussion.

Individuals and Organisations Interviewed, Surveyed, or Consulted by The Local Government Centre Research Team

Andrew Baird	Bathgate Area Initiative Team
Madame Eoanidis	Centre for Research on European Women
William Ley	COFACE
John Bell	Community Development Foundation
Gabriel Channon	Community Development Foundation
Kevin Harris	Community Development Foundation
June Lightfoot	Community Development Foundation
Charlie McConnell	Community Development Foundation
David Thomas	Community Development Foundation
Robin Bower	Community Service Volunteers
Stephen Crampton	Consumers in the European Community Group
John Knightly	Croydon Voluntary Action
Fran Jones	Cynon Valley Citizens Advice Bureau
Pat Bower	Cynon Valley CPA
Mark Latimer	Directory of Social Change
Elizabeth Drury	European Consultant
Alan Rees	Edinburgh Council of Social Services
Tony Venables	Euro-Citizen-Action Service
Margaret Batty	Eurolink Age
Jim Murray	European Bureau of Consumer Unions
Madame Paschner	European Environmental Bureau
Mary Collins	FEANTSA (European Federation of National Organisations Working with the Homeless)
Brian Harvey	Consultant
Mme Christine Louro	HELIOS Programme
Bernard Vanderhaegen	HELIOS Programme
Jeanette Longfield	International Heart Network
Don Flynn	Joint Council for the Welfare of Immigrants
Jacqueline de Groote	Lobby Européen des Femmes
John Harris	MENCAP (Wales)
Victoria Winkler	Mid Glamorgan County Council
Jane Goldsmith	National Alliance of Women's Organisations
Bob Smart	National Children's Homes
Sue Slipman	National Council for One Parent Families (also a member of the Economic and Social Committee)
Sarah Buchanan	National Council for Voluntary Organisations
Bill Seary	National Council for Voluntary Organisations
Dave Simmonds	National Council for Voluntary Organisations

Perri 6	National Council for Voluntary Organisations
Nigel Tarling	National Council for Voluntary Organisations
Jill Evans	National Federation of Women's Institutes (Wales)
Quintin Oliver	Northern Ireland Council for Voluntary Action
Alf Dubs	Refugee Council
Diana Robbins	Research consultant Social Welfare Policy & Practice
Steven Cooper	Royal National Institute for the Blind
Anne Stafford	RSPCC
Gill Alexander	Save The Children (Scotland)
Laurie Naumann	Scottish Council for Single Homeless
Susan Elsley	Scottish Council for Voluntary Organisations
Jim Jackson	Scottish Council for Voluntary Organisations
Stephen Maxwell	Scottish Council for Voluntary Organisations
Dot Pringle	Scottish Council for Voluntary Organisations
Usha Brown	Scottish Low Pay Unit
Agnes Ridley	Scottish Refugee Council
M Makrami	SHAKTI
Jonathon Stanley	Standing Conference on Racial Equality in Europe (SCORE)
Damian Killeen	Strathclyde Anti-Poverty Alliance
Peter Bryant	Welsh Council of Voluntary Action
Nia Wyn Thomas	Welsh Joint Education Committee
Alistair Grimes	WISE Group

Questionnaires Returned

Artlink, West Yorkshire
British Agencies for Adoption and Fostering
Brothers of Charity Services
Buckinghamshire Federation of Community Organisations
City of London & Hackney MIND
Community Council for Wiltshire
Community Council of Humberside
Dyfed Association of Voluntary Services
Exeter Council for Voluntary Service
Festival Welfare Services
Gatliff Hebridean Hostels Trust
Gloucestershire and West of England Training Initiative
Greater Manchester CVS
Heeley City Farm Trust, Sheffield
Hulme Study - Tenants
Kenton Youth and Community Centre

Leeds Health For All 2000
Manchester Alliance for Community Care
Methodist Church European Affairs Committee
National Community Health Resource
National Foster Care Association
Nottingham CVS
Shades City Centre Project, Manchester
South Kirklees CVS
Stockport Council for Voluntary Service
Transport for Leisure
Welsh Initiative for Specialised Employment
West Yorkshire European Business Information Centre
West Yorkshire Radio Action

APPENDIX C

HOW THE EUROPEAN COMMUNITY WORKS

Community Institutions

Information for this Appendix has been drawn from EC documents, *The Europe 1992 Directory: A Research and Information Guide; Grants from Europe: How to Get Money and Influence Policy*, and the Local Government International Bureau bulletins.

Diagram 1 gives an overview of the institutions of the Community and of their interrelationship.

Diagram 1

HOW THE EUROPEAN COMMUNITY WORKS

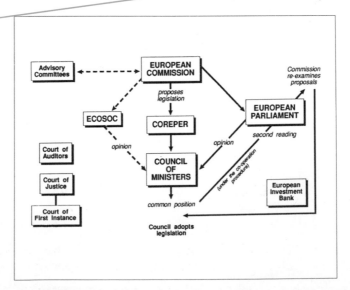

Source: *European Information Service*, Local Government International Bureau

European Commission

The European Commission is the executive arm of the Community with a role unique in intergovernmental organisations, being at once think-tank, civil service and referee. It is responsible for initiating and drafting legislation and for monitoring its application once adopted, and also for adopting secondary implementation measures itself. It consists of 17 Commissioners appointed by the member states: two each from France, Germany, Italy, Spain and the UK, and one from each of the other countries. However, once appointed, they must swear an oath that they will act independently of purely national interests. The two UK Commissioners traditionally come from the two major political parties, and for the 1989-1993 period were Leon Brittan and Bruce Millan.

Decisions within the Commission are taken by a simple majority vote, i.e. at least 9 out of the 17 Commissioners have to support a proposal.

The Commission is divided into 23 Directorate Generals covering the following areas:

DG I	External relations
DG II	Economic and financial affairs
DG III	Internal market and industrial affairs
DG IV	Competition (cartels) and state aids
DG V	Employment, social affairs, and education
DG VI	Agriculture
DG VII	Transport
DG VIII	Aid to developing countries
DG IX	Personnel, administration, and translations
DG X	Information, communications, and culture
DG XI	Environment and nuclear safety
DG XII	Science and research and development, including the Joint Research Centre
DG XIII	Telecommunications, information industries, and innovation
DG XIV	Fisheries
DG XV	Financial institutions, company law, and tax
DG XVI	Regional development and policy
DG XVII	Energy
DG XVIII	EC credit and investments (borrowing and lending)
DG XIX	EC budgets
DG XX	Budgets (internal financial control)
DG XXI	Customs Union and indirect taxation
DG XXII	Co-ordination of structural institutions and structural action
DG XXIII	Enterprise policy, commerce, tourism, and social economics

The Commission is based in Brussels and has a permanent staff of about 15,000 people. This is a relatively small civil service compared to the departments of most national governments, especially as 20 per cent of its staff are employed on translation and interpretation into the Community's nine official languages. The EC's staff is smaller, for example, than the Scottish Office.

DIAGRAM 2

EUROPEAN PARLIAMENT 1989

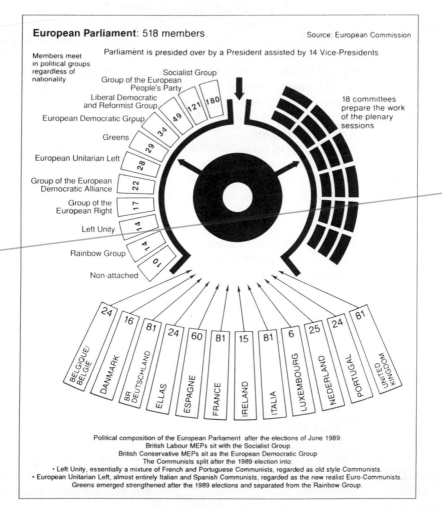

European Parliament: 518 members   Source: European Commission

Parliament is presided over by a President assisted by 14 Vice-Presidents

Members meet in political groups regardless of nationality

Socialist Group
Group of the European People's Party
Liberal Democratic and Reformist Group
European Democratic Group
Greens
European Unitarian Left
Group of the European Democratic Alliance
Group of the European Right
Left Unity
Rainbow Group
Non-attached

180 121 49 34 29 28 22 17 14 14 10

18 committees prepare the work of the plenary sessions

24 16 81 24 60 81 15 81 6 25 24 81

BELGIQUE/BELGIE · DANMARK · BR DEUTSCHLAND · ELLAS · ESPAGNE · FRANCE · IRELAND · ITALIA · LUXEMBOURG · NEDERLAND · PORTUGAL · UNITED KINGDOM

Political composition of the European Parliament after the elections of June 1989.
British Labour MEPs sit with the Socialist Group
British Conservative MEPs sit as the European Democratic Group
The Communists split after the 1989 election into:
• Left Unity, essentially a mixture of French and Portuguese Communists, regarded as old style Communists.
• European Unitarian Left, almost entirely Italian and Spanish Communists, regarded as the new realist Euro-Communists.
Greens emerged strengthened after the 1989 elections and separated from the Rainbow Group.

Source: Inglis, A. and Hoskyns, C. *The Europe 1992 Directory: A Research and Information Guide*, HMSO, 1990

European Parliament

The European Parliament is made up of 518 MEPs directly elected by the people of the 12 member states. Member states have different systems for electing their MEPs. Most use proportional representation, but in the UK, apart from Northern Ireland, voting takes place in a first past the post system in 78 large single member constituencies. In Northern Ireland three members are elected using a proportional representation system.

In the Parliament, members meet in political groups regardless of nationality. Diagram 2 shows the political composition of the Parliament after the 1989 elections.

The Parliament holds its sessions in Strasbourg. Its 18 Committees, which prepare the work for the plenary sessions and the political groups, meet for the most part in Brussels. The Parliament's general secretariat is based in Luxembourg.

Also important are the intergroups. These draw interested MEPs from all parties and all member states to examine in detail particular issues. Examples of intergroups are those on consumer affairs, the family, ageing, and disabled people.

Council of Ministers

The Council of Ministers is where final decisions are taken and legislation adopted. The Council consists of the relevant Ministers from the national governments of the member states, according to the subject matter under discussion. Thus there is an Agriculture Council, an Industry Council, a Transport Council, a Social Affairs Council, etc. The most general Council is the Council of Foreign Ministers which excercises general oversight of community affairs.

In addition to normal Council meetings, the European Council, comprising heads of state or heads of government, meets twice a year to discuss broad areas of policy, sometimes referred to as summit meetings.

Council meetings are chaired by the member state holding the presidency. The presidency is held by member states in rotation in alphabetical order of country. The presidency is held for six months.

Within the Council, decisions can be taken by unanimity, by simple majority voting, or by qualified majority, which is based on the relative size of the member states by population. Most single-market proposals are subject to 'qualified majority' voting. The list below gives the relative weights of the votes held by the member states under this system.

Member State	Number of Votes
United Kingdom	10
Germany	10
France	10

163

Italy	10
Spain	8
Belgium	5
Greece	5
Netherlands	5
Portugal	5
Denmark	3
Ireland	3
Luxembourg	2
TOTAL	76

For a measure to be adopted by a qualified majority 54 votes are required. A blocking minority is therefore 23 votes, i.e. a minimum of three member states.

Economic and Social Committee
The Economic and Social Committee (ECOSOC) has 189 Members nominated by the member states and consists of representatives of employers, workers and various interests. It is a purely consultative committee, giving its opinions on proposals, but it is the one formal body of the Community that can have voluntary sector representatives on it.

Committee of Permanent Representatives
The Committee of Permanent Representatives of the member states (COREPER) is made up of national civil servants, and is where the initial discussion of proposals takes place between the member states.

Court of Justice
The Court of Justice rules on any cases brought before it concerning the application of Community legislation, which takes precedence over national legislation in those subject areas under the Community's competence. It consists of 13 judges appointed for 6 years. The Court can hear complaints brought by individuals and can uphold the direct applicability of Treaty imposed principles eg on equal pay for men and women.

Court of First Instance
The Court of First Instance was created in 1988 to relieve the Court of Justice of some of the more routine cases concerning disagreements between the Commission and its staff and the application of the competition rules.

Court of Auditors
The Court of Auditors oversees the operation of the Community's finances.

European Investment Bank
The Bank provides loans on a non-profit basis for capital investment which helps to achieve the balanced development of the Community.

How Decisions Are Made

Decisions within the Community are made as a result of interactions between the Council of Ministers, the Commission, and the Parliament. The Commission has the right to propose legislation and the Council has the final right of decision. The Parliament has the power to reject the Budget, which it has done twice, and to remove the Commission, which it has never done, and until recently only had the right to be consulted on proposed legislation. However, under the SEA, a new 'co-operation procedure' has been introduced, which involves the Parliament to a much greater extent in the legislative process. The consultation and co-operation procedure are summarised in Diagram 3.

From this flow chart, it can be seen that if the Parliament rejects the Council's common position in the first instance, this can be overruled later by the Council acting unanimously. It is only after the lapse of a further period of time that the Council may act by a qualified majority.

The co-operation procedure applies only to some 10 articles of the EC Treaty but they include important areas, notably the bulk of legislative harmonisation necessary for the 1992 programme, specific research programmes, regional fund decisions, and some social policy matters. The old consultation procedure still applies to some measures within the 1992 programme, i.e. fiscal matters, free movement of labour, and measures involving workers' rights.

The Council acts by passing regulations, which apply as law in member states; directives, which require member states to achieve specified results but do not lay down the details of implementation; decisions, which are binding only on the particular parties concerned with a policy issue; and a miscellany of recommendations, opinions, resolutions and declarations, which have no binding power.

The Budget

Community spending in 1990 was about 48.8 billion ECU (about £34 billion), which was equivalent to approximately 1 per cent of the GNP of the 12 member states.

The budget is financed by the Community's own resources:

- customs duties and levies on imports from the rest of the world,

165

- a proportion of VAT collected in the member states.

- a new resource created in 1988 and based on the GNP of the member states.

DIAGRAM 3

CO-OPERATION PROCEDURE

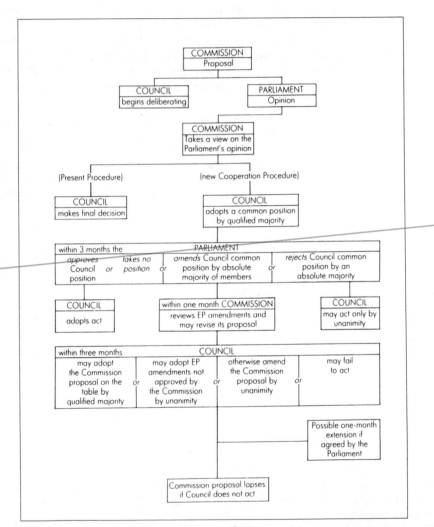

Source: Teague, Paul. *The European Community: The Social Dimension*, Kogan Page Ltd., 1989 (in association with Cranfield School of Management)

In 1990 the breakdown of expenditure was as follows:

- Support for farm prices, modernization of agriculture, fisheries — 59 per cent

- Regional policy — 12 per cent

- Social policy — 9 per cent

- Joint action in research, energy, industry, the environment and transport — 4.7 per cent

- Aid to Third World countries — 2.7 per cent

- Administrative expenditure, including staff salaries — 4.8 per cent

It is the Parliament which adopts the Community budget, unless it decides to reject it, in which case the budgetary procedure must be re-started. The budget is prepared by the Commission and goes backwards and forwards between the Council and the Parliament. In the case of obligatory expenditure (mainly agricultural expenditure), the Council takes the final decision. But with non-obligatory expenditure, the Parliament has the last word and can modify expenditure. Hence the importance of decisions on many individual budget lines in the Community budget which can authorise or amend whole areas of work being proposed by the Commission.

In the past there have been significant conflicts over the budget between the Council and the Parliament. However, in 1988 there was agreement to increase budgetary resources substantially, and an agreement which laid down overall budget limits until 1992, and these agreements have lessened the conflict to a considerable degree.

APPENDIX D

VOLUNTARY ORGANISATIONS IN THE EUROPEAN COMMUNITY

The following is an extract from an article by Diana Robbins entitled 'Voluntary Organisations in the European Community' (Voluntas, 1/2 Nov 1990). We are grateful to the author and to Manchester University Press for allowing us to reproduce a substantial section of the article here. It is a very useful summary of the role and structure of the voluntary sector in other European member states.

Belgium

The place of nongovernmental organisation (NGOs) in Belgian society reflects the very complex character of the legal and administrative framework, which is an inevitable consequence of the federal structure of the state. About three-quarters of the Belgian population are Catholic, and the traditional importance of the Catholic Church as a 'non governmental' provider of social assistance is still very marked, particularly in Flanders. But there have been big changes in the voluntary sector in recent years - changes which have an echo in a number of other EC countries.

The functions of NGOs in the social field are broadly as follows. They share with statutory authorities the implementation of state policy, and in some fields of social welfare they are the main, if not the sole, providers of services. Catholic organisations, for example, run an extensive network of hospitals, old people's homes, welfare centres and so on; and provision for psychiatric patients is almost wholly the preserve of the voluntary sector. Funding for these services is channelled through the Communities (the two main components of the Belgian state, plus the small German-speaking Community), and through local authorities. Their income also increasingly depends on the charges which are paid by people who receive their services.

Apart from this kind of role, which implies a very close relationship with the state, they play the part of experimenters and innovators. New kinds of need are identified by the voluntary sector organisations, and approaches to meeting new needs are pioneered by them. 'Experiments' which prove effective, and which achieve political and public approval, may be absorbed into the state/voluntary system of social welfare services. Examples of relatively new kinds of activity for Belgian NGOs include work on homelessness and addiction. They appeal directly to public opinion in order to generate support for the work they do, and in the context of the fight against poverty ATD (Aide à Toute Détresse) Fourth World is a very influential voice.

A number of different kinds of voluntary organisation are active in providing services for disadvantaged people, developing innovations in provision and in campaigning for state action on a range of issues. Catholic organisations have already been mentioned and, of these, the most important is Caritas. There are other parallel organisations providing services on a wide scale, which do very similar work from a different religious or ideological perspective - Socialist or Protestant organisations, for example. Apart from these, there is a very large number of non-profit welfare organisations which run social work centres, crisis centres, advice and counselling services, and so on. As in other countries of the Community, the economic crisis in Belgium has led to the demand for specific services linked to the needs of unemployed people; unemployment advice centres run by voluntary organisations have been established in many areas.

Volunteering has grown in importance, and there is a range of activities which are performed solely or mainly by volunteers - a telephone advice service for individual personal crises is one - or on a mutual aid basis. This is one of the signs of important changes within the voluntary sector. NGOs remain dominant in the provision of services and Catholic organisations are still the most important. But there has been an enormous growth in small, predominantly secular initiatives, as well as increasing interest in community development. The labour movement has become involved in campaigns to support unemployed people; and groups of independent professionals have come together to fill gaps in provision which they have identified. Self-help groups have formed to meet the needs of women and immigrant families.

The system of social assistance in Belgium has always depended on the voluntary sector, and has always been complicated. This complexity has led - in the view of some observers - to, at best, very fragmented provision for poor people which relies heavily on the informal care offered by families to vulnerable members. It is estimated, for example, that more than half the number of elderly people who need constant personal care are looked after by their families rather than by state or voluntary services. This informal, internal, sector of support and care is largely undocumented, but clearly remains a crucial factor in provision for some vulnerable groups.

Denmark

The so-called Scandinavian model of social welfare, which sees the state as the main or even sole provider, characterises the Danish system.[1] The government and the people of Denmark have insisted that arrangements for the support of vulnerable and disadvantaged groups should be rooted in legislation, funded by the state, and administered by the bureaucracy. NGOs remain relatively unimportant as service-providers. But, of course, the model implies other functions for the voluntary sector: as campaigners, advocates, and innovators.

There are a number of different kinds of voluntary organisation working in Denmark, almost all of which receive some public funding, some as much as 50-70 per cent of their funding.

(a)   The work of the big philanthropic and charity organisations dates back to the beginning of the century, when organisations such as the Church Army and the Salvation Army provided relief for destitute people. Today, the Church Army, for example, has a total annual budget of about 50 million Danish kroner, and although religion plays only a small part in the life of Denmark, church-based organisations - including the Young Men's Christian Association and the Young Women's Christian Association - are still the most important providers of emergency help to people in extreme difficulties. These organisations make use of paid staff and volunteers, but do not have a tradition of participation by the poor themselves.

(b)   Large, predominantly secular voluntary organisations were set up between the wars to protect the interests of particular client groups - disabled people for example. These NGOs have often been initiated by the relatives of clients, or by groups of concerned professionals. Until recently, few of them made any attempt actively to involve the 'target group' in the running of the organisations or design of policies. They typically monitor relevant state provision, campaign for improvements, provide information and pilot innovative kinds of service, sometimes with substantial public funding. Other sources of funding can include individual donations, trades union support, and contributions from private companies.

(c)   There has been a comparatively recent growth of grassroots, community organisations, usually based on self-help. This apparently spontaneous explosion of community action in the 1960s was linked to the development of the women's movement, and has parallels in other EC countries. Many of these groups are still concerned with the disadvantage and poverty particularly experienced by women. Others

- for example, the 'B-Team' ! operate as support and information networks among poor people, offering an alternative to conventional provision.

(d) Two other relatively new kinds of action are provided by the tenants' associations, which campaign on housing issues; and the trades unions, which traditionally were only concerned about the interests of employees, but have been driven by the economic crisis to consider the impact of unemployment in creating poverty.

Although the Danish voluntary sector is very varied, it is possible to generalise about their functions in relation to state provision.

- They do not replace state provision. Where they provide services, these are a supplement to existing provision to meet needs which may have been overlooked - for example, in relation to domestic violence or addiction - or to pioneering new kinds of service such as counselling, drop-in centres, and so on.

- They provide the impetus to innovation both through the service initiatives they take, and through their unremitting critique of conventional services. As pressure groups for particular interests, campaigners for change, and mobilisers of opinion - including the opinions of poor people - they are key actors in the process of social development.

- Their functions are reinforced by their capacity to operate in a qualitatively different way from the statutory sector in their contacts with disadvantaged groups.

The importance of NGOs in the Danish system has been underlined in the 1980s by government interest and encouragement expressed through the policy of 'privatising the public sector'. This differs from the process of limiting the growth of the welfare state in favour of commercial for-profit provision which has emerged in some other states, notably the UK. It has not been seen as an excuse to reduce public expenditure on social welfare, but as a means of attacking bureaucratisation and inflexibility, and of promoting experimental, innovative services. Similarly, the call for greater family responsibility - implying increased burdens for the informal sector of care - is not part of the Danish debate. Most Danish women work, and their right to do so has been recognised, for example, in the extensive state provision of day-care for children. Recent surveys, however, have shown that volunteering has an important place in Danish life. Most volunteers are young men from higher socio-economic groups, many committing a substantial number of hours to volunteer work.

171

France

In France, 'associations' are the equivalent of voluntary organisations, although their place in French political vocabulary is rather different from that of their counterparts in the rest of Europe.[2] There has been an enormous growth in membership of associations since the 1960s, although only a minority of this growth has been linked to concern for poor or vulnerable people. Associations provide the context for community action over a wide range of interests and issues, and increasing support for them has been linked to alienation from conventional politics, and the desire for a 'parallel', alternative kind of local political action. Volunteering has been relatively undeveloped in France, but the recent explosion of support for associations has aroused considerable official interest, as much for what the association offers to participants, as for any 'services' they may provide to others.

In 1984, it was estimated that about six per cent of all French adults were involved in associations which were broadly concerned with social welfare and mutual aid. This kind of organisation has its origins in the mutual aid associations which pre-date the 1901 law relating to freedom of association. At that time, there were estimated to be 2,259 associations, about half of which were concerned with health and social policy issues. By 1984, a report by the Inspector General of Social Affairs estimated that there were 90,000 associations active in the social field, with between seven and eight million members. They provided 550,000 places in institutions and services, employed some 290,000 people, and had an estimated annual turnover of 465,000 million francs in 1982. These figures relate to the whole range of organisations: big Catholic and national charities like the Red Cross, and influential federations of voluntary groups like UNIOPPS, right through to very small groups wholly dependent on the work of volunteers.

By 1986 the Economic and Social Council recorded a total of between 500,000 and 600,000 associations, of which about one-third were broadly concerned with health, education and social welfare. In the health field, voluntary organisations were important, not so much for the hospital places they provided (about 17.5 per cent of the total), as for the community-based provision in which they took the lead. In the field of social welfare provision, their contribution was crucial. They provided 51.6 per cent of all 'capacity', including 80 per cent of all institutional places and services for handicapped people, 70 per cent of domiciliary services, 28 per cent of old people's homes, 6 per cent of sheltered housing, 80 per cent of holiday accommodation for disadvantaged families and 18 per cent of creche places. And the associations providing these services - some 7,000 - were estimated to be less than one-tenth of the associations active in one way or another in the health and social welfare fields. Information about the rest was scarce, but they were thought to have an important function in the formulation of policy, especially at local level, and included family associations, organisations active in the fight against poverty, and pensioners' groups.

Apart from the actual provision of social welfare services, which is clearly a very important role for some associations in France, NGOs are seen as innovators - developing initiatives which may then be taken on by statutory services, and bringing to light gaps in provision - as well as advocates and campaigners. They are also seen, more generally, as social mediators, occupying the middle ground between different political spheres: social and economic, public and private, paid and voluntary. And finally, they are described in some official accounts as presenting an important context for the development of political, social and personal relationships between citizens, and for the encouragement of the social inclusion of groups which might otherwise be marginalised.

The Economic and Social Council made a number of recommendations in 1986 (Conseil Economique et Social, 1986) designed to encourage the voluntary sector, and a report on volunteering in 1989 (Cheroutre, 1989) continued the emphasis of the intrinsic value of voluntary activity to the health of the state. The recommendations included the extension of tax advantages for associations, assistance with management and training, removing obstacles to volunteering, and suggestions for strengthening the links between public and voluntary institutions.

Federal Republic of Germany

In most of the FRG, voluntary organisations predominate in the provision of social welfare services for disabled, disadvantaged, and vulnerable people. They have a long history in Germany, and a unique legal status which is based on the 'subsidiarity principle'. This principle, basic to German social welfare policy, implies that the state has a duty to intervene in an individual's situation, but *after* the alternatives have been exhausted. These alternatives include, first, the support of the individual's family and community, and, second, services offered by the voluntary sector. The increasing cost of social welfare has led to growing official emphasis on self-help, and large numbers of self-help activities have developed during the 1970s and 1980s. There were an estimated 22,120 self-help groups active in 1985. Many of them have been sponsored by trades unions: others have their origins in the student movement of the 1960s, and have little sympathy with the subsidiarity principle, which is nevertheless the basis on which they are able to claim some state support.

Since the Middle Ages, the 'relief of the poor' has been the responsibility of the Church, and of voluntary welfare agencies. While the state now has overall responsibility for welfare, priority is still given to voluntary provision, and the subsidiarity principle gives voluntary organisations a strong claim on public resources while protecting their independence from state control. The law provides that the statutory authorities cannot set up a service if an adequate voluntary alternative exists, but they can invite an NGO to set up an institution or service for them. The work of state and voluntary agencies in many areas is genuinely complementary, and professionals move between the two types of institution or service in the course of their careers. The state is the junior partner in provision in the whole of the FRG, apart from Berlin, Bremen and Hamburg. Apart from public and non-profit services, there is a growing commercial residential sector, catering mainly for more affluent elderly people: about 76,000 elderly people were estimated to be living in this kind of institution in 1986.

There are six main umbrella organisations which co-ordinate the voluntary sector at national level, which together make up the 'Federal Association of Voluntary Welfare Agencies', an influential body which is routinely consulted about social legislation. Each of the six has a different religious or ideological base, but they perform roughly similar functions:

- The Federal Workers Welfare Association, based on the Social Democratic Workers' Movement, was estimated in 1988 to have about 588,000 members.

- The Service Agency of the Protestant Church in Germany draws its members from the Service Agencies of 17 member churches, 10 free churches and 100 specialist associations.

- The German Caritas Foundation, like the Caritas associations in other EC member states, is a major welfare association with a large full-time staff.

- The German Non-Denominational Welfare Association supports and co-ordinates the work of self-help groups through 10 independent regional associations. Its membership has increased considerably in the past decade.

- The German Red Cross is the largest national assistance agency in the FRG, and had 4.71 million members in 1988, of whom about 343,000 were active members.

- The Central Welfare Office of the Jews in Germany was re-established in 1951, and concentrates on community social work for elderly people, as well as work with the young and with refugees.

The annual income of NGOs was thought to amount to 2.4 per cent of NGP in 1985. Apart from public funds, the voluntary welfare agencies all contribute a proportion of their own funds, which they raise from a number of sources, including individual donations and levies on congregations. In 1987 the six organisations listed above were responsible for more than 60,000 social institutions, including hospitals, youth welfare and family assistance centres, agencies catering for the needs of elderly and disabled people and people in 'special social situations', and training centres for social and community workers. About 750,000 professional staff worked in these agencies - two-thirds full-time and one-third part-time - and about 1,500,000 unpaid voluntary workers helped to run them. By far the largest proportion of NGO effort goes into hospitals: the six organisations were responsible for about 23,000 hospitals in 1987, employing about 262,000 staff.

Critics of the system point to the confusing diversity of provision, which can have the effect of denying access to services, as well as to the increasingly bureaucratic procedures which it involves. Thousands of community-based groups have emerged in the late 1980s, providing local alternatives to the very 'public' character of established voluntary provision. These initiatives have not always been welcomed by social service professionals who see the growth of the self-help movement as playing into the hands of those who would like to reduce the part played by the state in the provision of welfare and the fight against poverty.

Greece

Social action and assistance in Greece have tended to emerge in times of crisis - to deal with the effects of wars, civil disruption or natural disasters. The national system is still rather limited, very centralised with Athens as the 'centre' of the whole of the country, and relatively unco-ordinated. The family and the Church - traditional sources of support for poor, vulnerable or dependent people - remain very important.

Since the 1950s there has been a determined expansion of state welfare provision, with a corresponding decline in the importance of NGOs. Nevertheless, the picture for the country as a whole shows a wide variety in the kind and extent of services for less advantaged groups. Typically, a local area will depend on a mixture of some state and more voluntary provision, the latter usually related to a church organisation and, in some areas, NGOs may be the only resource apart from the family.

A number of the big charitable organisations operate at a national level, including the Red Cross, the Young Men's Christian Association and the Young Women's Christian Association. They provide specialised advice services, social work, help in the community for disabled people, and training for volunteers. At a local level, there will be a whole range of small associations - often based around the local church - to deal with local needs.

175

NGOs are seen as less bureaucratic, more flexible and innovative than state services, and recent evidence of this was provided by their development of community-care centres for elderly people, which were subsequently taken over by the state.

Provision for special needs in Greece has tended to mean institutions: for elderly people, people with disabilities and children in need of care. At the beginning of the 1980s, one survey estimated that church and other voluntary groups accounted for up to 40 per cent of places in residential care for children, 96 per cent in homes for elderly people, and 70 per cent of beds for people who were physically handicapped, and virtually all for people who were mentally handicapped, was provided by NGOs. They are often part-funded by the state, which may also participate in the management of particular programmes. In 1986, for example, 56.5 per cent of NGOs' budgets were provided by the state, 6 per cent came from fundraising, and 9 per cent came from charges made to users of services.

There has recently been a move towards 'nationalisation' of the network of voluntary institutions. Between 1981 and 1986 the revenues of NGOs increased by 245 per cent, while the comparable figure for state agencies was 357 per cent and between 1984 and 1988 the number of public institutions increased by 404, and the number of NGO-run establishments declined by 10, mostly in the residential child-care sector. This reflects concern about the coverage and consistency of provision which NGOs are able to provide, as well as anxieties about their funding and accountability. Some observers, however, have seen this development - which has gone alongside a reduced rate of increase in funding to NGOs - as leading to a deterioration in services, which in turn has encouraged the commercial sector to increase its share of residential provision, and some services such as reception centres for returning migrants. In Greater Athens, for example, there are known to be about 40 'private enterprise' homes for elderly people, charging fees which make them accessible only to the more affluent Athenians.

The growth in private, for-profit provision may also relate to the beginnings of change in attitudes to the family and to the caring role of women. In 1983, for example, the total capacity of all residential provision for elderly people which was also virtually the *only* kind of provision accounted for 0.5 per cent of the elderly population. Clearly, most of the care of infirm elderly people was being provided by the traditionally very strong caring networks of women. Although they remain important, projects funded under the Second EC Programme to Combat Poverty reported that these networks could no longer be taken for granted: the notion of the extended family was becoming more restricted as more women needed and looked for paid work outside the home.

Very little is known about the extent of volunteering in Greece. It is thought to be relatively undeveloped, partly because of the attitudes to the family which have already been mentioned, and because of the prevailing view that it is the state's responsibility to provide services to supplement family care. Volunteering is generally identified with philanthropy and traditional forms of charitable action, and church and other NGOs tend to involve volunteers in fund raising rather than service provision.

The weaknesses of the existing system, and the place of NGOs in it, were described in an official report in 1985 (Greek Ministry of National Economy, 1985, pp191-2, 383-7). It called for decentralisation, better co-ordination and distribution of services, a greater degree of participation by the public in their design and organisation, development of community-based provision, and a 'holistic' approach to the problems faced by poor people. Many of these criticisms were reinforced by Greek projects working in the Second EC Poverty Programme. One new element in the welfare mix which is developing is provided by groups of professionals who are establishing new kinds of secular, voluntary provision to fill gaps in the existing system.

Ireland

In common with other predominantly Catholic countries in Europe, Ireland has to this day a pattern of social policy and community action which reflects many of the traditions of the Church towards family care, service and charity.[3] One of the largest Catholic charities - the Society of St Vincent de Paul - has about 1,000 local branches throughout Ireland, and about 10,000 members, and has been described as operating 'a shadow welfare state', which covered not just social welfare services but also included some income maintenance work.

The historical dominance of Catholic organisations in meeting demands for care and support which could not be covered by the family continued into the 1960s. It was taken for granted that church-based NGOs would run institutions, provide services and co-ordinate parish welfare activities. The religious orders were the principal providers of hospitals and schools, and were also active in the fields of child care and care of the elderly. Services for people with mental and physical disabilities were developed by Catholic agencies, who are still the most important organisations in this field.

The character of the Irish NGOs and their place in the social system began to change in the early 1970s as a result of a number of factors: criticism of the scale and distribution of state provision in the context of the 'rediscovery of poverty': an increasing emphasis on the rights of poorer citizens, as opposed to the client approach of traditional charity work; and the critique of the burden of family care from the women's movement. Voluntary organisations with a campaigning approach were emerging, which made use of techniques of community development and the language of community empowerment.

And the 1980s saw the development of self-help groups, again partly as a result of the stimulus of the women's movement.

Discussion of the voluntary sector in Ireland, as in other member states, is hindered by lack of information and difficulties of definition. Nevertheless, it seems clear that the traditionally important role of the Church as the provider of social welfare services continues. These services receive the majority of their funding from the state, but church organisations are also bound to raise a significant proportion of their own funding. At the same time, new kinds of NGO are fulfilling different functions and developing different kinds of relationship with statutory services. The range of voluntary activity includes specialist residential services for the elderly, handicapped and chronically ill people, run by religious orders; major national Catholic and secular organisations, working particularly in the fields of mental handicap and disability; voluntary organisations concerned with campaigning, action-research and community-based provision for special needs, for example, homelessness, delinquency and addiction; activities based on growing trades union interest in the fight against poverty; self-help groups, focused on a range of needs; and local social service organisations based on the village and parish. Of course, this list is not exhaustive and does not take account of the many thousands of small voluntary groups which meet community interests in sport, leisure, the environment, and so on.

In the field of social welfare, and welfare rights for poor people, some aspects of the existing situation have given rise to concern. Observers point to the proliferation and unevenness of provision; to the preponderance of charity as the basis of assistance, and of the medical model in institutional care; and to the lack of co-ordination and training available to the voluntary sector, and to that sector's heavy dependence on state funding. On the other hand, the past two decades have seen exciting innovations in the voluntary field, not just in terms of the initiatives which groups have taken in, and on behalf of, the community, but also in terms of the forms of association which are developing.

Italy

There are at least five elements at work in Italy providing services and care for poor, disabled and vulnerable people. The first is the state, of course. Second is the family, which remains an important resource, despite demographic change, changes in the age structure of some populations due to migration, and the role of the women's movement in drawing attention to the unacceptable burden of care which the traditional family structure could imply. Third, there is private, for-profit provision, a currently limited sector, but one that could grow in importance to fill the vacuum left by the changing family. At present, commercial interests are concentrated on homes for elderly people, residential accommodation for psychiatric patients, and leisure facilities. Fourth, and importantly, there are voluntary organisations, including Catholic organisations and other big charities, as well as new forms of NGO. And, finally, there is the volunteer movement which is basic to social action and social welfare in Italy.

Formal social service provision is distributed through local government, following a strong commitment to decentralisation which was put into practice by the Italian state in the 1970s. The Catholic tradition of service and care has given the Church a complementary role in social welfare. Many church-based organisations are active and, although figures are not available, many of the familiar social institutions are run by the big Catholic charities, such as Caritas. Linked to this tradition, but not entirely explained by it, is the growth in volunteering which - although again not fully documented - has been a marked feature of the Italian situation in the past 10-15 years.

The volunteer sector is particularly hard to define and quantify. A social survey undertaken in 1985 showed that 1,400,000 Italians dedicate an average of seven hours a week to voluntary work, not all of this, of course, in the social welfare field (Italian Ministry of Internal Affairs, 1985, p.74). 'Volunteering' can include participation in sports groups, trades unions, and trade associations. But one survey of 15,000 groups engaged in voluntary work in 1985 showed the following breakdown: 34.4 per cent concerned with welfare; 24.2 per cent concerned with culture; 21.1 per cent concerned with education; and 20.3 per cent concerned with health (Milan Istituto per la Ricerca Sociale, quoted in Charities Aid Foundation, 1990). These percentages give some impression of the large numbers of people who give their time voluntarily to support the health and welfare services. In general, they do not *replace* services provided by the state or the traditional charities, but they offer complementary activities; for example, assistance in hospitals, domiciliary care for people who are disabled or terminally ill, and community centres for under-privileged groups. Since a large proportion of the resources devoted to the formal system of social welfare is consumed by large institutions, these kinds of initiatives have been an important addition to community-based provision.

It has been estimated that nearly half the volunteering organisations in Italy were set up since 1977; and one survey found that the hours volunteered had increased by more than 40 per cent between 1981 and 1984. Because of the recent and remarkable growth in *voluntariato* in Italy, it is tempting to see it as a single movement, but in fact it represents a range of different kinds of activity. Some volunteers are attached to the traditional kind of institution, run by state or charity. Others work in the more innovative kinds of provision which some Catholic organisations and local authorities are pioneering. Many more form part of the growing number of volunteer associations which are developing services for special-needs groups, sometimes in direct partnership with local authorities, in the context of philosophies of self-help or community empowerment.

The process of decentralisation and the existence of many different kinds of agency working in the field of social welfare and the fight against poverty have combined to produce - in the view of some observers - an unacceptably fragmented and confusing system. Others criticise the emphasis on large institutions; still others point to the predominance of 'charity' rather than a system based on welfare rights. The increase in volunteering has certainly been one response to these factors. Another has been the emergence of a new kind of NGO, often based on the concerns of a small group of professionals, who organise flexible, community-based services at the same time as trying to modify the traditional institutions and achieve an equal voice in policy discussions with the public sector.

Luxembourg

Key factors which determine the role of voluntary agencies in Luxembourg are: first, the relative affluence of the country and its low level of unemployment; second, its history as a crossroads in Europe resulting in a very varied population and culture; third, the importance of the Catholic Church and its principles of charity and welfare; and finally - and perhaps this is the most important factor of all - since the late seventies, NGOs have worked within a very closely structured relationship with the state.[4]

Government departments - especially the Ministry of the Family - have established agreements with the main voluntary organisations involved in work with disadvantaged groups, which provide state funding for salaries and running costs and some collaboration in management and monitoring, but allow the NGOs freedom to determine and work towards their own objectives. How real this 'freedom' can be in the context of total funding has been disputed, and some observers believe that the kind of contract which the voluntary sector has with the state in Luxembourg must result in bureaucratisation, and distance from poor people.

On the other hand, there are clear advantages in terms of co-ordination, accountability, and certainty of continued provision. Despite their closeness to the state, NGOs have not lost their capacity to draw attention to gaps in provision and develop new ways of filling them. If state funds are not available for a new initiative, voluntary organisations may raise funds through individual donations or from charitable foundations. Once a project has established the value of a new approach or service, the organisers may ask for state funding or may be invited by the relevant Ministry to develop and extend their work. Another advantage attributed to this system is that, even when they are operating state-funded services or distributing state benefits, charity or other non governmental workers are thought to be less threatening to poor people.

A number of different kinds of non-profit, voluntary organisation can be distinguished in the poverty field in Luxembourg. There are big Catholic charities - the most important are Caritas, and the Society of St Vincent de Paul. (Even Caritas' work is funded by the state to the tune of 80 per cent, which gives some indication of the degree of state funding which other organisations enjoy.) ATD Fourth World also has considerable influence on public opinion, and is seen by some as providing the 'conscience' behind state action on poverty and disadvantage. Then there are some national voluntary organisations, such as l'AMIPERAS (an organisation concerned with the needs of elderly people). Older people are an important political constituency in the country, since they form the largest wholly-indigenous age group, and the influence of l'AMIPERAS reflects this.

Grassroots community groups or self-help groups are very rare, but there are small-scale associations working to meet particular needs, which may not receive immediate state funding and depend on local, popular support. Trade unions are not a significant factor in the welfare field, since they have chiefly been concerned only with workers native to Luxembourg.

The services for vulnerable groups which are run by voluntary organisations include: residential-care homes and day centres for elderly people; day care for infants and children; residential care for children and young people; night shelters for homeless people; family support services; projects for disadvantaged immigrant groups; day centres for disabled people; training and drop-in centres for unemployed young people; and projects for lone parents, and the victims of domestic violence. In addition, major charities, such as Caritas, collaborate in the administration of the guaranteed minimum income system.

The relationship between the private, voluntary sector and the state in Luxembourg is rarely one of confrontation, but is generally characterised by co-operation in a relatively crisis-free context.

The Netherlands

International comparative studies which hope to draw a sharp contrast in styles of social system very often refer to the situation in the Netherlands as the opposite extreme from, say, the situation in some Scandinavian countries. In Sweden, for example, state agencies account for virtually all provision for disadvantaged groups, and the role of the voluntary sector as a service provider is negligible. But in the Netherlands, this position is reversed: the majority of 'public' services in the social field are provided by NGOs. In this kind of context, where voluntary organisations are implementing state policy and receive nearly 90 per cent of their funding from the state and from compulsory insurance (nearly 100 per cent in the case of homes for the elderly, and the provision of personal social services), it is important to identify how they differ from public agencies.

One source of difference derives from the fact that they serve different constituencies, which in turn relates to the history of the Dutch social system. In the Middle Ages guilds operated a kind of welfare system for members, leading to a very varied pattern of provision which persisted to the nineteenth century. At the same time, at the beginning of this century, strongly felt religious and political allegiances meant that the design of the modern Dutch social state was bound to take account of the extreme cultural and ideological differences in the population.

The result today is a wide variety of church-based and secular organisations running hospitals, schools, cultural activities and social welfare services, as well as a large (but unknown) number of small community-based and self-help groups serving particular interests. One example of this variety can be demonstrated in the field of homelessness. In 1989, it was estimated that there were 19 official organisations working on homelessness in the Netherlands, about 90 relevant policy initiatives, some 500 hostels run by charities, and 1,000 commercial hostels, as well as smaller pressure groups, self-help groups and projects directed at particular homeless populations.

It is estimated that the total gross expenditure of NGOs in 1982 amounted to some 15 per cent of GNP. The main headings of NGO expenditure were as follows: education (37 per cent of total expenditure); health (32 per cent); and social services and provision for elderly people (15 per cent).

Despite the heavy reliance of the state on NGOs for the provision of services, and the dependence of the service-providing voluntary sector on state funding, the relationship between the public and the independent, non-profit institutions in the Netherlands has not become cosy or complacent. There are about 12 national action groups representing people who are dependent on state benefits, which campaign for improvements to the system; and - as in other parts of the Community - ATD Fourth World works to support the poor and promote political recognition of their situation. In fact, many of the major NGOs are involved in campaigning and advocacy, and one church organisation (DISK) has developed the technique of 'adopting' particular Members of Parliament in order to monitor and influence their attitudes and actions.

Again, in common with some other member states, the Netherlands has seen a sharply increasing bill for social welfare provision, which has encouraged government interest in self-help, and community-based provision rather than residential care. Solidarity within families and neighbourhoods has been promoted by means of the official campaign in favour of a 'careful society', but little is known about the extent of the informal sector, or about the capacity of the modern family and community to re-absorb some of the responsibilities which have been performed by the state.

Portugal

The system of social welfare which predated the revolution of April 1974 in Portugal depended to a large extent on Catholic organisations which had been active in the field since the fifteenth century. Church-based NGOs - the Misericordias - were responsible for social assistance of all kinds, with the support of the Monarchy, into the nineteenth century. They still exist, after a period of nationalisation followed by reprivatisation, and are developing a new role in the new social state.

The new Constitution of 1976 committed the state to organising, supporting, co-ordinating and funding a unified and decentralised social service system. It was to be a mixed system, allowing the development of non-profit 'private institutions of social solidarity' alongside improved and extended state provision. Like Spain, the Portuguese state confronted economic crisis almost simultaneously with new and increased expectations from the population in the social welfare field, and this gave particular importance to the future role of the voluntary sector.

Today, NGOs supplement state provision in a number of policy areas related to disadvantage and poverty. Many of them are linked to the Catholic Church, but there are also large and growing numbers of secular voluntary organisations and community groups. In 1984, the breakdown of responsibility for key social welfare services was as follows: children and young people (public, 17.5 per cent; private, 76.0 per cent); invalidity and rehabilitation (public, 17.8 per cent; private, 82.2 per cent); elderly people (public, 17.4 per cent; private, 79.4 per cent); other (public, 14.0 per cent; private, 85.0 per cent). In the same year, more than 50 per cent of public expenditure on social welfare was allocated to the voluntary sector, compared with about 33 per cent to the public sector.

It was estimated that at the end of 1985, there were about 1,784 NGOs in Portugal actively involved in social welfare, co-ordinated through regional centres. Four-fifths of all services for children and elderly people were run by NGOs and between 1982 and 1985, public funding for the voluntary sector increased by about nine per cent a year in real terms. Other sources of income for the voluntary sector included individual donations, charges for services (at a level set by the state for state-funded activities) and income from property.

One exception to the prevailing welfare mix is the city of Lisbon, where social services are the sole responsibility of the Santa Casa da Misericordia de

Lisboa. Originally a private non-profit organisation, the Lisbon Misericordia now enjoys an ambiguous status since its activities are closely controlled by government, and its services are regarded as inseparable from state policy and funding.

In the late 1980s, the relationship between the public and private sectors were again the subject of debate in Portugal, and the balance is still in a state of transition. Family and neighbourhood solidarity remains strong, but can no longer be taken wholly for granted. Volunteering of the traditional kind associated with Catholic charities continues. 'Self-help' as the basis of social action is relatively unknown. The sort of action-research which was promoted as part of the Second EC Programme to Combat Poverty was also new to much of Portugal, and stimulated new approaches to social policies, and to groups with problems which conventional services ignored.

Spain

There are no global figures to describe the full extent of voluntary, non-profit and volunteering activity in Spain. But it is clear that the enormous changes in Spanish social policy, following the break with the Franco regime and the introduction of the new Constitution in 1978, have had an equally dramatic impact on NGOs and their role in relation to less advantaged groups.

The family in Spain, in common with other EC countries of the south, has traditionally been and remains the most important source of support and care. It is still expected, for example, that young unemployed people will be housed and supported by their families. The growth in the women's movement during the 1980s has called into question the caring capacity of the family, but it is still largely taken for granted by policy.

Apart from the family, the big Catholic charities used to be the only providers of care for some vulnerable groups: for example, for young people in trouble with the law, and people identified as addicts or vagrants. But in the period following the political upheaval of the late 1970s their approach was strongly criticised as stigmatising and reinforcing the marginal position of poor people. During Franco's last years, local grassroots voluntary activity tended to be channelled into the demand for political change and the establishment of state services. The achievement of many of these changes led initially to reduced activity at local level, as activists were absorbed by participation in new political and administrative structures.

A number of factors have continued the process of change over the past decade:

(a) Decentralisation and local autonomy, which has combined with increased emphasis on participation to encourage the development of community-based services.

184

(b)   Demand for a 'welfare-state' approach, which would provide services for all, without stigmatising the poorest groups.

(c)   The economic recession, which has both increased the demand for services, and encouraged the state to look for ways of limiting the escalating cost of provision through new forms of partnership with the non-governmental sector.

A new and crucial role for the traditional charities has evolved in response to these pressures. Caritas remains the most important voluntary provider of social welfare, and the Red Cross is also very active. With other Catholic organisations - such as the monastic orders which have traditionally been important in the fields of health care and education, and local parish groups - they now complement and support the very new statutory social welfare provision. They also are beginning to compete with them, in the sense of developing new kinds of service or exposing gaps and deficiencies in existing provision.

Although details and figures are not available, it is known that there has been a surge of grassroots activity in the late 1980s which hof community-based associations, and in an increased emphasis onparticipation in the design and administration of services. elf-help has not traainst poverty in Spain, but ideas of self-help and mutual d have been developed by growing numbers of the women's org operate traditional networks. Volunteers participate in providing the whole range of social services. One recent survey of voluntary organisations in Catalonia showed that 57 per cent of people who volunteered worked with handicapped people, 18 per cent with families, children and young people; 5 per cent with elderly people, and 2 per cent in the field of drug dependency (Charities Aid Foundation, 1991).

The kinds of partnerships evolving between statutory and voluntary agencies in Spain are based on the traditional role of the family and a very new role for 'charity'. Interest in and support for the development of a welfare state remains strong; but economic factors are pressing the state to look at forms of welfare pluralism which will reinforce the importance of the voluntary and volunteering sectors.

United Kingdom

A number of traditions have combined in the history of the very large, varied and active voluntary sector in the UK.[5] One of these is the Victorian ideal of charity, and traditional charities are still represented, often associated with the Church. In this century, in parallel with the development of the welfare state, organisations have grown up to defend and promote the interests of different target groups, press for better provision, publish information and provide supplementary or innovative services. 'Self-help' and mutual aid have their origins in the labour movement, and have become especially important in the context of equal opportunities for minority ethnic groups and for women. Government programmes - for example, the Community Development Projects and the Urban Programme in the 1960s and 1970s, and more recently a series of programmes aimed at training young people which channelled funding to the voluntary sector through the Manpower Services Commission - have had the effect of encouraging the growth and significance of the voluntary sector in the design and implementation of public policy.

The so-called Poverty Lobby, which has campaigned since the 1950s on behalf of and with disadvantaged groups in British society includes a number of different kinds of organisation. It is often difficult to pin down precisely where the energy behind a particular campaign has originated: with the trades unions or the women's movement, with grassroots community action, or with research. Some of the main NGOs working in this field are well-known, such as the Child Poverty Action Group and the Low Pay Unit, and remain important in monitoring the impact of public policy on poor people, and stimulating debate and action. Pressure groups come together to work on specific issues, often in conjunction with the big national campaigning authorities. An important source of co-ordination in the sector is the National Council for Voluntary Organisations, which provides up-to-date information on funding and legislation, advice on management and development, a forum for networking among voluntary organisations, and a point of contact and consultation with central and local government. Another network which became of increasing importance during the 1980s was the parish system of the Church of England, which began to take a new approach to the deprivation to be seen in inner-city areas based on the rights of citizens rather than charity.

It is impossible to be precise about how many voluntary organisations are active in the UK. One estimate for the 1970s put the figure at more than 350,000 (Gerard, 1983). It is easier to be clear about the number of bodies which have the legal status of 'charities', but it is important to remember that not all charities are concerned with under-privileged groups, and campaigning voluntary organisations may be refused charitable status because of the prohibition against political activities. More than 160,000 organisations are registered as charities, and this total has increased steadily throughout the 1980s. Their estimated income amounted to 4.1 per cent of GNP in 1985, derived from the following sources: fundraising and donations (15 per cent); fees and charges (60 per cent); rents and investments (11 per cent); grants from statutory bodies (11 per cent); and commercial activity and other (2 per cent).

The voluntary sector as a whole relies heavily on public funding, which has increased substantially during the 1980s, but which now appears to be levelling off. Dependence on central funding, which may be linked to policy

186

goals at variance with the underlying aims of some NGOs, and on local funding which has begun to be increasingly restricted, has given rise to anxiety and debate about the independence, accountability and security of a sector which supplies crucial services and employs many thousands of professional staff. Many, but not all, voluntary organisations in the UK make use of the work of volunteers in running their services, and commonly use volunteer help to raise funds. One recent survey (Charity Household Survey, p.26, *Voluntas*, Volunteer Centre, quoted in Charities Aid Foundation, 1990) showed that about 44 per cent of respondents had undertaken some kind of volunteering activity in the previous month.

NGOs in Northern Ireland play a particularly vital role in sustaining the community, and in developing services which correspond with needs. The voluntary sector in the whole of the UK has monitored and participated in the very extensive changes to the social state which have resulted from years of government by a political party committed to reducing state intervention, and introducing market values to service provision. Some of the implications of these changes are summarised here.

New kinds of unelected 'intermediate bodies' - such as the Urban Development Corporations, or Training and Enterprise Councils - have been set up by government, and they provide part of the local, quasi-statutory context in which NGOs now have to work and compete with the commercial sector. The role of local government in relation to NGOs has changed during the decade. Local authorities continue to provide important support, despite a series of laws which have reduced their powers in the social field (for example, in housing, education and inner-city development). Legislation now before Parliament, on the other hand, will give local government sweeping new powers to support and develop the voluntary sector in the field of personal social services and care in the community for vulnerable groups. The growth of the 'contract culture', which gives NGOs a chance to compete with for-profit organisations in providing services, also highlights their importance as advocates and intermediaries on behalf of vulnerable citizens whose needs may be disregarded or overruled.

CONCLUSION

Two main points stand out from this necessarily brief and incomplete overview of the role and activities of voluntary organisations in the countries of the Community. First, no account of the social welfare provision in each state is complete without an assessment of the scale and value of the voluntary sector. Even at national level, information is very scarce, and few attempts have been made to quantify the contribution of the voluntary element in the social welfare mix. Quantification does not, of course, imply devaluing the qualitative strengths of the voluntary sector, which also deserves much more thorough exploration and evaluation.

The second, related, point goes back to the European Commission's social agenda. In the absence of national data, and definitions which can form the agreed basis for cross-national comparison, the full welfare implications of the single market cannot be predicted or understood. Discussion of the rights of workers, the needs of the less advantaged, of migration and 'social dumping' is all taking place in the vacuum left by incomplete information about existing systems. There is a clear and urgent need for coordinated action by the Community institutions to stimulate the collection of national data, according to consistent definitions; and to promote a programme of the kind of coherent, cross-national research which will complete the picture of the voluntary sector which is presented only in outline here.

NOTES

1   Much of the information about Danish NGOs derives from papers written by Professor Peter Abrahamson at the University of Roskilde.

2   Jean-Clause Barbier, Deputy Director of Research at the Caisse Nationale des Allocations Familiales, Paris, has kindly supplied many of the documents on which this section is based.

3   Papers written by Seamus O'Cinneide, St Patrick's Collee, Maynooth, formed the basis of this section.

4   Information about Luxembourg was principally supplied by Dr Claudia Hartmann-Hirsch, CFFM, Luxembourg

5   Apart from material from the National Council for Voluntary Organisations and Charities Aid Foundation in London, I am particularly grateful for working papers supplied by Professor Martin Knapp and his colleagues at the PSSRU, University of Kent at Canterbury, England.

REFERENCES

1   Charities Aid Foundation (1990) *Charity Trends*, 12th Ed, Tonbridge, Kent, England.

2   Cheroutre, Marie-Thérèse (1989). 'L'essor et l'avenir du bénévolat, facteur amelioration de la qualité de la vie', *Journal Officiel de la République Française*, 12 July, Paris.

3   Conseil Économique et Social (1986). 'Avis adopte par le Conseil Economique et Social', *Journal Officiel de la République Française*, 29 July, Paris.

4   EUROPHIL Trust (1990). *Voluntary Bodies in the European Community*, EUROPHIL Trust, Interphil House, Yalding, Kent, England.

5   Gerard, D. (1983) *Charities in Britain: Conservatism or Change?*, Bedford Square Press, London. Quoted in NCVO Information Sheet 6a, rev edn, January 1990.

6   Greek Ministry of National Economy (KEPE) (1985) *Programme for Economic and Social Development*, Athens.

7   Italian Ministry of Internal Affairs, Civil Service Department (1985), *Social Assistance and Social Security in Italy*, Rome.

8   VUSEC Report (1986) *Voluntary Work and Unemployment Study in the Countries of the European Communities*, Official Publications of the European Communities, Luxembourg. Available through HMSO, London.

APPENDIX E

A GUIDE TO KEY LITERATURE

General

Crampton, S. 1992 *Eurospeak Explained*. Rosters Limited, London. Gives explanations for more than 500 terms used in connection with the Community.

Davison, A. and Seary, B. (1990) *Grants from Europe*. Bedford Square Press, London. A good guide to sources of money within the Community. Gives details of programmes and of contact points.

European Community (1990) *1992 - the Social Dimension*. A summary by the Commission of action in the Community social area, with discussion about present and future policy developments.

Grahl, J. and Teague, P. (1990) *1992 - The Big Market: The Future of the European Community*. Lawrence and Wishart, London. A useful introduction to the issues, including chapters on the social dimension, the regional dimension and Britain and the European Community.

Inglis, A. and Hoskyns, C. (1990) *The Europe 1992 Directory: A Research and Information Guide*. HMSO, London. This is not a regular bulletin, but in addition to providing basic information about the EC and 1992, lists useful sources of information, including a number of bulletins and newsletters.

Lodge, J. (ed) (1989) *The European Community and the Challenge of the Future*. Pinter Publishers, London. A collection of essays, many of which are detailed, referring to the acts, regulations, and directives. Gives a historical perspective on each issue.

Palmer, J. (1989) *1992 and Beyond*, Office for Official Publications of the European Communities, Luxembourg. Examines the political debate about the future of the Community. Concentrates on economic matters, including the debates about world trade and monetary union, but also includes discussion of enlargement, relations with Eastern Europe, the democratic deficit and the creation of a citizens' Europe of social and political rights.

190

The Voluntary Sector in European Member States

Harvey, B. (1992) *Networking in Europe: A Guide to European Voluntary Organisations*. NCVO Publications (incorporating Bedford Square Press), London. This book will include a country by country study of the voluntary sector in the 11 other EC countries, mapping its main features, how it is different from the UK voluntary sector, and how voluntary organisations can make contact with it. It will also include a brief tour of the emerging voluntary sector in central European countries and the USSR.

Robbins, D. (1991) 'Voluntary Organisations and the social state in the European Community', *Voluntas* 1:2 pp.98-128. A clear summary of the main features of the social welfare systems operating in each of the 12 member states. A section of this article is included as an appendix to this report.

Local Government

Bongers, P. (1990) *Local Government and 1992*. Longman, Harlow. A short guide to the organisational, functional and socio-economic impacts of 1992 on local government. A good introduction to the issues facing local authorities.

Roberts, P. et. al. (1990) *Local Authorities and 1992*. Centre for Local Economic Strategies, Manchester. This report has chapters on competition policy, economic development, labour markets and social measures, public procurement, transport and environmental policy.

Economics and Employment

Cecchini, P. (1988) *The European Challenge, 1992: The Benefits of a Single Market*. Wildwood House, Aldershot. Outlines the results of the research on the economic effects of the Single Market. Focuses on the benefits of industrial restructuring and the removal of barriers to trade.

European Commission (1990) *Employment in Europe*, Office for Official Publications of the European Communities. A guide to employment trends throughout the Community and to the employment programmes of the Community. Well presented with lots of tables and diagrams.

Neuberger, H. (1989) 'The Economics of 1992', *Local Government Policy Making*, December 1989. Critically evaluates the Cecchini conclusions.

Rajan, A. *1992 A Zero Sum Game: Business, Know-How, and Training Challenges in an Integrated Europe*. Industrial Society Press, London.

Analyses business changes and labour market challenges and outlines a way forward in the areas of education and training.

Regional Policy

Cheshire, P. (1990) 'Explaining the Recent Performance of the European Community's Major Urban Regions', *Urban Studies*, 27, 311-333.

PA Cambridge Economic Consultants Ltd. *The Regional Impact of Policies Implemented in the Context of Completing the Community's Internal Market by 1992.* A short report for the European Commission which looks at the effects of completing the internal market on sectors and regions of different types.

Social Welfare and Poverty

Abrahamson. P. (1991) *Welfare and Poverty in the Europe of the 1990s: Social Progress or Social Dumping?*, Roskilde University, Denmark.

Benington, J. (1990) *Local Strategies to Combat Poverty: Lessons from the 2nd European Programme to Combat Poverty*, Working Paper 4, The Local Government Centre, University of Warwick.

Berghman, J. (1990) 'The Implications of 1992 for Social Policy: a Selective Critique of Social Insurance Protection' in Mangeen et al (eds) *The Implications of 1992 for Social Insurance.* Cross-national research papers, LSE.

Room, G. et al (1987) *Action to Combat Poverty: the Experience of 65 Projects.* First report of the programme evaluation team. Centre for the Analysis of Social Policy, University of Bath.

Walker, C. and Walker, A. (1987) *Poverty in Great Britain*, National Contextual Paper for the second European Poverty Programme. Available from CASP, University of Bath.

Wilson, G. (1990) Caring and the Welfare State in the 1990s in Hantrais et al (eds) *Caring and the Welfare State in the 1990s*, Cross National Research Papers, LSE.

Elderly People and Ageing

Eurolink Age Bulletins are published three times a year by Eurolink Age. Covers specific EC developments of interest to elderly people, as well as

192

broader social welfare developments, EC policy on disability, consumers, poverty, etc., and has a regular section on 'beyond the Europe of 12'.

Family Policies in the EC

European Observatory on National Family Policies (1990) *Families and Policies: Evolutions and Trends in 1988-1989* Commission of the European Communities, DGV. Also available from Institut de l'enfance et de la famille, 3 Rue Coq-Heron 75001, Paris. A useful summary of data and policies of relevance to families in each member state of the EC.

Homelessness

FEANTSA (1989) *European Action against Homelessness*. First seminar of the European federation of national organisations working with the homeless. FEANTSA, rue Defacq 1, boite 17, 1050 Bruxelles, Belgium.

Disability

HELIOS Newsletters are produced free of charge in all nine official community languages as part of the HELIOS network funded by the EC. A useful summary of all the Commission's activities in the field of disability.

Black and Ethnic Minorities and Refugees

Dummett, A. (1990) *Europe and 1992: Focus on Racial Issues*, Catholic Association for Racial Justice, London. A short pamphlet focusing on racial issues, including racial equality, freedom of movement, migration and the rights of third country nationals and refugees.

Gordon, P. (1989) *Fortress Europe? The Meaning of 1992*, The Runnymede Trust, London. A pamphlet that examines immigration policies being developed in Europe and their likely effects, especially on refugees. It warns of the dangers of the rise of a new Europe-wide racism.

JCWI (1989) *Unequal Migrants: The European Community's Unequal Treatment of Migrants and Refugees*, Joint Council for the Welfare of Immigrants, London. Reviews policy on rights of entry for migrants and refugees.

Civil Liberties

Spencer, M. (1990) *1992 And All That: Civil Liberties in the Balance*, Civil Liberties Trust, London. A useful guide to all the main civil liberties issues including 'Fortress Europe', data protection, policing Europe, social Europe and human rights. Argues the case for a civil liberties lobby.

Women and Childcare

Cohen, B. (1990) *Caring for Children: the 1990 Report*. Report for the European Commission's Childcare Network on childcare services and policy in the UK. Family Policy Studies Centre.

Conroy Jackson, P. (1990) *The Impact of the Completion of the Internal Market on Women in the European Community*. Prepared for the Equal Opportunities Unit of DGV of the EC V/506/90/EN.

Crawley, C. (1990) '1992 and its effects on women'. *European Labour Forum*, autumn, pp.44-46.

Finch, J. (1990) 'Women, Equal Opportunities and Welfare in the European Community: Some Questions and Issues' in (eds) O'Brien, M. Hantrais, L. and Mangen, S. *Women, Equal Opportunities and Welfare*, Cross National Research Papers, Aston University, Birmingham.

Goldsmith, J. (1990) *Summary of Preliminary Study of the Impact of the Creation of the 1992 Single European Market on Black and Ethnic Minority Women in the UK*. National Alliance of Women's Organisations, London.

Grant, J. (1990) *1992: Women and Europe. Opportunities and Dangers*, National Alliance of Women's Organisations.

Moss, P. (1990) *Childcare in the European Communities 1985-1990, Women of Europe* supplement 31, CEC, Brussels.

Whitting, G. (1990) 'Women and 1992: Opportunity or Disaster?' in Manning, N. and Ungerson, C. (eds) *Social Policy Review*, Longman, London.

Health

Hodgkin, C. (1991) '1992 - Is Harmonsiation Healthy?' *Critical Public Health*, 1991, 1, pp.11-17.

National Community Health Resource (1990) '1992: How will it affect local communities?' *Community Health Action*, November.

The Public Health Alliance. *1992 The People's Health - Who's in Charge?* A report of a conference held to explore the relationship between public health and Europe.

MacCarthy, M. (1991) 'Health Care in the European Community - The significance of the single European market'. *Critical Public Health*, 1991, 1, pp.6-10.

Environment

Haigh, N. and Baldock, D. (1989) *Environmental Policy and 1992*, Institute for European Environmental Policy. A report prepared for the Department of the Environment which examines the environmental components of the SEA, measures proposed by the Commission and the environmental pressures that will be caused by the economic consequences of 1992.

Robins, N. (1990) *A European Environment Charter*, Fabian Society, London. This examines the environmental record of the Community and makes suggestions for tackling the 'green deficit', including proposing the adoption of an Environment Charter and an Environment Fund.

Consumers

European Commission (1990) *The European Community and Consumer Protection*, European File 14/90. A basic guide to past policy in this area and an outline of the action plan for 1990-1992.

Consumers in the European Community Group (1987) *Could Do Better: Towards an EEC Policy for Consumers*, CECG, London. A short document outlining improvements that CECG would like to see in EC work for consumers.

Consumers in the European Community Group (1990) *Annual Report*, CECG, London. A guide to the issues that CECG are pursuing on behalf of consumers.

Regular Bulletins and Newsletters

EuroNews (previously *Euromonitor*) is a bulletin about Europe and 1992 specifically for the UK voluntary and community sectors. Produced collaboratively by six organisations: the Charities Aid Foundation, the Charities Tax Reform Group, Community Development Foundation, the Directory of Social Change, the Legislation Monitoring Service and the National Council for Voluntary Organisations. Published about three times a year. Freely distributed by the Directory of Social Change, Radius Works, Back Lane, London, NW3 1HL.

European Information Service is a monthly bulletin produced by the Local Government Information Bureau, specifically for local authorities. Extremely clear and possibly the most comprehensive guide to recent developments within the EC. Available from LGIB, 35 Great Smith Street, London SW1P 3BJ.

The Week in Europe is a weekly newsheet produced by the Commission of the EC. Available from CEC Offices, Jean Monnet House, 8 Storey's Gate, London, SW1P 3AT.

The European Citizen is a monthly bulletin produced by the European Citizen Action Service. Produced specifically for voluntary organisations in Europe, with a focus on helping the voluntary sector present their case and to lobby more successfully in Europe. ECAS, Rue du Trone 98, 1050 Brussels, Belgium.

APPENDIX F

LOCAL AUTHORITIES AND THE VOLUNTARY SECTOR: THE EXAMPLE OF MID GLAMORGAN COUNCIL

Mid Glamorgan County Council, like a growing number of local authorities in the UK, takes the European Community seriously.

There are a number of reasons for this:

- the EC is an important Centre of decision-making - we need to monitor legislation and lobby when necessary;

- the Single European Market brings both opportunities and threats - we need to ensure that the people of Mid Glamorgan are well prepared;

- the EC can provide financial support for certain projects - we need to maximise grant aid for good schemes.

In recognition of this, the County Council has provided staff and resources to ensure that the people of Mid Glamorgan benefit from the EC. They include:

- two specialist staff with expertise in EC matters

- access to the services of a firm of consultants based in Brussels

- a comprehensive range of literature by and about the EC

- contacts with key UK and EC officials

Whilst the County Council's own needs must be priority, these resources are also available to organisations with complementary aims working in Mid Glamorgan.

What We Can Do

1   Indicate the main sources of EC Funds.

2   Provide technical advice on the 'Structural Funds'.

3   Provide access to relevant legislation, background literature, etc.

4   Help with interpreting 'Euro-jargon'.

5   Help to find the relevant UK or EC official.

6   Advise on applications for funding.

What We Can't Do

1   Search for EC money for your group's project.

2   Provide a general introduction to the EC.

3   Complete application forms.

4   Provide help with travel costs.

Some Examples

Over the last 18 months Mid Glamorgan County Council has helped a number of voluntary groups. For example:

- we have helped Rhondda Community Development Association to set up an exchange of young people with an Arts organisation in Berlin, and advised them on funding;

- we have advised local enterprise agencies (Merthyr and Aberdare Development Enterprise and Ogwr Partnership Trust) on sources of funding for training schemes, and helped them to prepare applications;

- we have advised local Groundwork Trusts on sources of funding for environmental improvements and helped them to prepare applications;

- we have produced a Guide to Sources of Funding for Educational Visits and Exchanges;

- we organise or contribute to seminars on EC matters such as 1992, the European Social Fund, the European Coal and Steel Community, Women in the EC (forthcoming), and regenerating coalfield communities.

INDEX

acid rain 128
additionality 60, 82
Ad Hoc Working Group on Immigration
   101
aerospace industry, cross-national
   initiatives for 64
ageing, of European population 75-6, 84
Agricultural Fund 66
agriculture
   changes in 52-3
   decline of jobs in 50
AIDs research, EC funding for 119
AIRLINE *see* aerospace industry
anti-poverty network, European
   (EAPN) 87-8
anti-poverty work in UK
alternative EC models for 88
   EC funding for 88
asylum seekers, in EC 95-7
Auditors, Court of 164

Belgium, voluntary organisations in
   168-9
black and ethnic women, particular
   disadvantages of 105-6
border controls, British attitude to
   abolition of 97
Bristol One Parent Project (BOPP) 88
budget (1990) of EC, items of interest to
   voluntary organisations 24-5

campaigning by voluntary organisations, at European level 149-51
Cecchini Committee, economic research
   by 11
Cecchini Report 11, 54, 127, 134-5, 143-4
CHANGE (Charities and Non-Profit
   Groups in Europe) 40
charities
   British, different from European 42-3
   fiscal privileges of 34-5, 43
   loss of VAT zero-rating for 148

Chernobyl disaster 126
childcare
   importance attached to by Commission
      104
   literature on 194
childcare   facilities,   possible
      improvements in 106
'Childcare   Now',   European
      campaigning by 111
Children Act (1989) 32
children in poverty, increase in numbers
   of 75
civil liberties, literature on 194
   work of 111
Coalfields Communities Campaign 60,
   64 *see also* RECHAR
Coalfield Communities Fund 60
COFACE (European Network of family
   organisations) 138
Combined European Bureau for Social
   Development 37
Comité Européen des Associations
   d'Intérêt General (CEDAG) 37
Commission 161-2
   action and research programmes
      supported by 20-1
   Citizens' Advisory Service of 34
   funding by for voluntary organisations
      41
   measures by to implement Social
      Charter 20
   powers and work of 22
   relations with voluntary organisations
      41-2
   watching briefs of 21
Common Agricultural Policy (CAP)
   consumers' concern over 138-9
   significance of for health 120
Commonwealth Immigration Act (1962)
   94-5
community care, voluntary sector's role
   in 32

199

occupational structure, future, in Europe 57-8

Overseas Development Institute, report on effects of 1992 27

Palma Document 96, 97

parental and family leave, EC draft directive on 108

part-time workers, draft EC directive on 108

Permanent Representatives of the member states, Committee of (COREPER) 164

pharmaceutical industries, countering work of by health pressure groups 120

pharmaceutical products, standards of control of 135

Pilton (Edinburgh) Project, partnership in 81

policy-making in EC, changes in 147-8

political union, target date for 22

pollution 126-9

poor in Europe, over-representation of women among 104

population of Europe, changes in 75-6, 84, 144

Portugal, voluntary organisations in 183-4

poverty in Europe
  change in profile of 72-5
  EC research into 83
  effect of European integration on 70-90
  EC programmes to combat 20, 80-3
  increase in EC 73-5
  literature on 192
  multi-dimensional aspect of 82

Poverty Observatory 83

poverty programmes of EC 20, 80-3
  additionality in 82
  EC funding for 82-3
  economic and social integration of 82
  interagency strategy of 82
  participation in by local communities 81-2
  partnership in 81

poverty in UK, high level of 73, 75

pregnant women, employment rights of, EC draft directive on 108

pressure-group organisations, opportunities for in Europe 36

prices, effect of single market on 135, 136

products, range of available in EC 135

Programme of Regional Action on the Initiative of the Commission concerning the Environment (ENVIREG) 130

Public Health Alliance
  conference held by on single market 121
  WHO Europe funding for 121

public health campaigns, funded by EC 118-9

public health movement in UK, European focus of 123

public sector contracts, increased competition for 34

Racial Equality in Europe, the Standing Conference on see SCORE

racism in Europe
  Council of Ministers declaration on 98
  European Parliament committee on, recommendations of 98-9
  growth of 98

RECHAR programme of EC 60, 66

Refugee Charter for Europe 99

Refugee Council, manifesto of 99

Refugee Forum, refugee charter produced by 99

refugees
  in EC 94-101
  literature on 193

regional basis, for EC-funded voluntary sector programmes 65-6

regional policy, literature on 192

regionalisation, within EC 65-6

RENAVAL programme of EC 59, 66

research for this book, individuals and organisations interviewed 156-9

RESIDER programme of EC 59

road freight, increase in 127

Rome, Treaty of see Treaty of Rome

rural development schemes, in EC 59, 62-3

SPEC employment creation programme 63

Structural Funds of EC 18, 148
  growth in cross-national programmes of 66

subsidiarity, principle of 26, 130, 146-7

SYSDEM programme 62

tobacco growing industry, EC subsidy for 120

tobacco lobby in EC 120-1

tobacco products, EC policy on 117-8

tourism, harmful effects of 127

town-twinning programmes 64

trade barriers, gains from removal of 12

training programmes of EC, major 62-3

Treaty of Rome 8-9
  social provisions of 84

Trevi Group 95, 101

unemployment
  long-term, programme to combat 62
UK
  high level of poverty in 73, 75
  projected job losses in 54-5
  refusal of to adopt Social Charter 18
  voluntary organisations in 185-7

UK consumer movement 137-8

UK Poverty Forum 87

unemployment, possible increase in 78

unemployment groups, self-help, links with European groups 64

United Kingdom see UK

urban environment, EC Green Paper on 129-30

USDAW (Union of Shop, Distributive and Allied Workers), report by 116

VAT rates, harmonisation of 135

VAT relief for charities, possible loss of 34-5, 148

voluntary organisations
  in Belgium 168-9
  British, different from European 42-3
  campaigning by at European level 149-51

co-ordinating, opportunities for in Europe 36-9

in Denmark 170-1

in EC 168-88

EC funding for 148

economic activities of 42

EC's view of 40-3

effect of new EC laws on 148-9

effect of single market on 33-40

in Federal Republic of Germany 173-5

in France 172-3

functions of 33-40

fund-raising function of 39-40

funding for by European institutions 41

in Greece 175-7

importance of European networks to 150

in Ireland 177-8

in Italy 178-80

legal changes affecting 35

in Luxembourg 180-1

new opportunities for in single market 147-50

in Portugal 183-4

pressure-group function of 35-6

relations with European institutions 41-2

resource and co-ordinating function of 36-9

self-help and mutual-aid function of 39

service-providing function of 33-5

in Spain 184-5

status of in Europe 42

in The Netherlands 181-3

voluntary organisations concerned with environment, need for action by 133

voluntary sector
  literature on 191
  role in EC 87-90

voluntary sector in UK
  challenges to 31-2
  expanding role of 32
  increasing involvement of in EC issues 121

Volunteurope 38

welfare, mixed economy 41-2, 147

207